Physicians In Transition

Doctors Who Successfully Reinvented Themselves

Volume 1 (Episodes 1-25)

by
Richard Fernandez, MD, MPH

Edited by Laura Lee Carter
Cover by Nick Zelinger

50 Interviews: Physicians in Transition: Doctors Who Successfully Reinvented Themselves (Volume 1)
Copyright © 2010 by Richard Fernandez
http://doctors.50interviews.com

ISBN: 978-1-935689-07-2
Library of Congress Control Number: 2010934845

Published by
Wise Media Group
444 17th Street, Suite 507
Denver, CO 80202
www.wisemediagroup.com

WISE
MEDIA GROUP

Based on original *50 Interviews* concept by Brian Schwartz.

First edition. Printed in the United States of America.

Dedications

I am dedicating this book - my very first book to my loving and understanding parents - Jennie and Benny Fernandez who always encouraged my dreams and supported their son the doctor.

They are enjoying my new career as an author and continue to support their son as an author.

These two people always stressed dream it, plan it, and do it.

FOREWORD

This is more than a book about physicians in transition.

This is a book about remarkable people who have overcome obstacles in the pursuit of personal happiness and career satisfaction.

Most physicians entered the medical field believing that sacrifices were inevitable but that the hard work and dedication would lead to a successful and satisfying career. Most people think the term "physician" implies the ultimate professional career choice. Why aren't physicians happy? What obstacles prevent them from this personal and career fulfillment?

The world of medicine is in flux. Health reform is threatening to increase the number of patients and further cut physician reimbursement. More and more doctors are seeking employment within a health system. The results of a recent Medical Group Management Association (MGMA) survey found that the three biggest challenges for physician group practices, in order, are rising operational costs, managing finances with uncertain Medicare reimbursement rates, and selecting and implementing a new electronic health record system.

For some physicians, the stress levels have progressed to the point of exhaustion and fatigue and in more severe cases, substance abuse or severe depression. Forty percent of doctors are burned out.[1] A survey done by The Physician's Foundation found that 78% of physicians think that medicine is "less rewarding" and 49% physicians will reduce the number of patients they see over the next three years.[2]

---

[1] Shanafelt, T., Balch, M., Bechamps, G., Russell, T. et al. "Burnout and Career Satisfaction Among American Surgeons". Annals of Surgery Vol.250 No.3 September 2009 p.463-471.

[2]Commins, John. "Unhappy Docs Provide Roadmap for Recruiting, Retention". HealthLeaders Media December 2008.

Think, for a moment, about what you would do. Consider that you've had 20+ years of schooling and are coming upon your third or fourth decade of life without having had the time, the resources or the opportunities for exposure to anything but one discipline. Pile on top of that the fact that you have paid thousands, sometimes hundreds of thousands of dollars to be in this place. Now imagine your anxiety, anger, frustration, fear and guilt as you realize the job satisfaction and personal fulfillment are sorely lacking.

Would you feel trapped? Like you'd lost yourself somewhere along the way? Maybe that you were a failure?

That's what I felt like.

It's very hard to find one resource that gives doctors the practical advice and planning tools to use his or her medical knowledge outside of traditional day-to-day clinical care. It's almost impossible to bring together the multiple resources necessary for the task. There is no defined path outside of traditional clinical medicine for a doctor. There are associations out there, websites one might stumble upon with the correct Goggle keyword search, a smattering of people across the country who specialize in helping doctors find satisfaction in their work or, if it comes to it, a non-clinical career.

This book will introduce you to individual doctors who felt lost, trapped, exhausted, sick, guilty, frightened and an array of other emotions. These doctors may not have understood the feelings or the root cause of the problem but they faced it head on, got through it and overcame the feelings.

Most of these doctors don't feel like they have done anything extraordinary or that they have now found their "perfect job". But each has demonstrated the courage to take the first step forward towards personal and professional satisfaction and fulfillment. Some of these doctors have taken miles of steps forward.

This is a diverse group of men and women coming from a variety of geographic locations, medical schools and training. They are from different specialties and at various stages of clinical experience. They share a common decidedly optimistic spirit and a unique balance of empowerment, hope and strength.

No matter how a doctor chooses to serve in this world, clinically or non-clinically, he or she will always be a doctor. Personally, that took me a long time to come to peace with. Through interacting with thousands of other doctors who fall along the spectrum of steps forward towards personal fulfillment and career satisfaction, I've come to believe it is a part of our identity and always will be. This is a good thing.

Enjoy this collection of profiles that challenges old ways of thinking about life and career as a doctor as we enter a new era of healthcare delivery in America.

You will be inspired!

Michelle Mudge-Riley, D.O., MHA
President, Physicians Helping Physicians
www.phphysicians.com
mudgeriley@yahoo.com

CONTENTS

Dr. David Best, CEO & Co-Founder 1

Dr. Mark Browne, Physician Executive.................................... 11

Dr. Jonathan Cargan, President, Freelance Author, Consultant 17

Dr. Lisa Chu , Musician, Life Coach, Entrepreneur 27

Dr. Kenneth Cohn, Author, Founder, Cancer Survivor............ 33

Dr. Jay Crutchfield, Surgical Arts... 47

Dr. Zoe Deol, Freelance Guru... 57

Dr. Robin Dhillon, Trainer, Consultant, Living with MS 67

Dr. Harry Greenspun, Chief Medical Officer 71

Dr. Alan Jacobson, Navy Veteran - Operation Desert Storm... 81

Dr. Philippa Kennealy, The Entrepreneurial MD 89

Dr. Joseph Kim, Physician Technologist 103

Dr. Michael McLaughlin, Author and Co-Founder 111

Dr. Ola Medhat , Physician Advisor.. 123

Dr. Rita Meek, Medical Director 127

Dr. Michelle Mudge-Riley, The Doctor's Doctor 139

Dr. Gabor Oroszlan, Senior Marketing Manager................... 145

Dr. Mary Padilla, Cytopathologist 149

Dr. Gail Reilly, Transitional Medicine 155

Dr. Angela Scharnhorst, Health Services Administrator 163

Dr. Mark Schnitzer, International Trainer............................... 167

Dr. Andrew Schwartz, Holistic Clinician 173

Dr. Kelly Sennholz, Founder, Chief Medical Officer............... 181

Dr. Rebecca Winokur, Senior Clinical Content Editor........... 193

Dr. Brian Young, Medical Writer and Consultant 201

"It is better to follow the voice inside and be at war with the whole world, than to follow the ways of the world and be at war with your deepest self."

- Michael Pastore

1

"I don't want a job where I can say what I will be doing thirty years from now on Tuesday afternoon."
Dr. David Best, CEO & Co-Founder

Despite being born and raised in Camden, New Jersey, David went on to Franklin and Marshall College, Temple University School of Medicine for his MD, Lenox Hill Hospital for his surgical residency, Pitt for ENT, and Baruch College for his MBA. He entered the world of pharmaceuticals in 1982 with Klemtner Advertising, a division of Saatchi and Saatchi, where he served as medical director and Senior Vice President, Account Supervisor. Subsequently, he was Medical Services Director for Bristol-Myers Squibb and on July 10, 1989, started the first scientifically credentialed Medical Science Liaison group. He went on to create Colleague Medical for Elsevier and in 1995 returned to Saatchi and started BESTMED, a medical education company. Combining all of the experience and creativity, David is now the President and Co-founder of MD*ea*, Inc., a novel medical education company. MD*ea* consists of a promotional medical education company (www.MDeaNY.com), a contract medical science liaison organization (www.MDeaNY.com/MSLs), a CME company (www.BetterCME.com) and also produces internet TV for doctors at TheDoctorsChannel.com.

DR. DAVID BEST

Q. Why did you decide to leave clinical medicine?

A. I felt a passion to leave and do something different, but I didn't have to leave. It was a simple interest to go into medicine in the first place. I was brain-washed from an early age by my Jewish mother. One day, when I was five, she cut her finger and said: "Dr. David, can you put a band-aid on this for me?" In spite of my brainwashing, I did find I had a lot of respect for my family doctor. He was a Marcus Welby type. When he spoke we'd listen, and when you didn't feel good, you hung onto every word. You were so glad to see him. He was the ideal doctor.

With that kind of influence, I thought I would like being a doctor too. Then I found my biology classes in high school and college very dry and boring, but I kept giving myself another chance. I went to med school. The first two years of basic science were not very interesting to me, and my clinical years weren't terrific either. When I did general surgery, I thought, "This is my specialty, I'm really going to love it." When that didn't happen, I said to myself, "This is not what I want to do for the rest of my life."

I would tell everybody, I don't want a job where I can say what I will be doing thirty years from now on a Tuesday afternoon. Most physicians agree with me. It becomes very rote no matter what area of medicine you go into. An open heart surgeon plays the radio in the operating room doing bypass surgery, because after you've done a couple of them, it's the same thing over and over again. A dermatologist gets bored seeing the same skin condition over and over again. No matter what you do.

Finally, I got so depressed, that I wrote a letter to thirty advertising agencies, saying that I was a physician with creative writing abilities and perhaps, "my interests are germane to your needs." I did it on a whim, and I did get some nice responses. Some invited me for interviews. The CEO of Comp-

CEO AND CO-FOUNDER

ton Advertising (now Saatchi and Saatchi), sent the letter down to their creative director at a medical agency. At that time, I didn't even know medical advertising existed.

The next thing you know they offered me an interview. I didn't respond for two months. When I finally wrote back and said, "Is that job still open?" They said, "Yes, we've been looking for a medical director for nine months." I flew there the very next day with my yearbook from medical school in hand. I had been the editor-in-chief. I interviewed and demonstrated my creativity using the yearbook and two weeks later I got the job. Those were the days when it was rare for a physician to be willing to work in advertising, or even consider leaving medicine. It was a rare thing back in 1982.

Q. Were you able to just leave cold? Or did you still continue some clinical medicine?
A. I had to soften it up a little bit when I told my parents. I told them at an Italian restaurant on Mulberry Street, Angelo's. They had all white tiles. I figured if there was any bloodshed they could wipe the walls down. My parents came from the depression era. My father said to me at graduation, "I always wanted to be a doctor's son, and the day you became one, I became one." So it was pretty tough to tell them I had decided to leave medicine. I think I said I was going to continue to work in the emergency room on Saturdays, just to keep my hands wet.

The rest is history. I absolutely love my career. It's been a wonderful twenty-eight years since I left my residency. I've tried medical administration, I've been on the advertising side, I've been on the client side, I worked for a pharmaceutical company, I worked in medical publishing for Elsevier, I had my own medical education company, part of Saatchi and Saatchi for ten years, and started a new med-ed company too.

DR. DAVID BEST

I recognized that I need to be continually reinventing myself. I need to continually think of new ways to reach my audience, especially when it's physicians. It has become more and more difficult to get the doctor's time and attention. Thus, we started a doctor's channel which is internet TV for doctors. We realized that nobody's attention span is longer than 2 minutes. In an age of media snacking, everybody gets their information in fragments throughout the day, whether its RSS news feeds, email on their Blackberry or YouTube on their phone.

We decided that the audience that has the least extra minutes in a day is the doctor. Our whole concept is to deliver information to physicians in one to two minutes, getting right to the point. We provide Information that doctors need to know delivered by colleagues and the world's experts. Years ago you could invite doctors for a weekend symposium at a resort and have their time for six hours a day, or invite them to three hour dinner meetings. Now, everybody wants to get their information online. They google it, and the next thing you know they have their answer. That is our concept, watch a short video by an expert, and quickly gain the most relevant information.

Q. Would you say that was one of your biggest breakthroughs, discovering that short attention span audience?

A. I don't want to take credit for this as a breakthrough. I think we were more gutsy than inventive. No one believed you could get a message across in one or two minutes to a physician. But that's what they've been asking for all these years. Reps still walk into the doctor's office and say, "Hey Doc, you got a minute?" We decided if the doctor does have a minute, let's give him something short but very valuable. The doctor does not have to make very much of an investment. If he/she doesn't find it interesting, he can click it off. When you go on YouTube, do you click on a nine minute video? No. You click on a 1:48 minute. Google research shows that 114 seconds is

CEO AND CO-FOUNDER

the optimal length for a video for most people. Doctors are probably a third of that. We love to say, "Editing is good manners." If you are sensitive to their time constraints, you will gain their acceptance. If you accept that the doctor's time is valuable, and you cater to that, they will come to you with open arms. That is why "The Doctor's Channel" has become so popular with thousands of views by doctors.

Q. What do you see in the future along the same communication lines?

A. I think people will probably catch up with this notion. No longer are you going to have an hour symposium with a camera in the back of the room broadcasting a talking head. We all get our information online on demand, and that will continue to grow. I also see an increased use of mobile devices. That is where we will get our information in the future. I think 78% of all doctors have a Smart phone now, and that will only continue to increase.

Doctors are ahead of consumers on online video watching, but that doesn't mean they are watching Star Trek online. They are apt to watch online educational videos, and they are clicking on topics that are delivered quickly and on demand. They are ahead of the general consumer on online video consumption. I think the future is in mobile devices in areas like video, getting CME certification through mobile, whether it is the iPhone or iPad. When doctors have some downtime, walking the dog or sitting at home, they look at a video on their iPhone or iPad or any mobile device. I think that is the future. None of us want to sit through long and tedious lectures anymore. I think everybody, whether a doctor or not, wants a little pearl delivered quickly and to the point.

Everybody loves lists: Top Ten Business Hotels, Top Ten Hottest Gadgets, Top Ten Biggest Sales on Amazon. Everybody responds to lists. Even the New York Times and the world

DR. DAVID BEST

5

of reporting have 'The Most Emailed Story.' That is social media. What made it most popular and most emailed is the group. It doesn't mean everybody is chatting about it. It means how many people sent it or clicked it or whatever. That is social media. The society decides what is the most important information for me to see right now.

Q. If I might step back a little to speak to doctors who are considering a job transition, it sounds like you were gutsy about it, and after that it all went pretty well. Not too many obstacles or tough areas?

A. I guess it was best that I didn't listen to my family or friends. The first thing they say when you say you are leaving the practice of medicine is, "Why don't you set up a practice first and try that? Then, if you don't like it..." But that involves is a large investment in time and money. I think the gutsy part is saying, "No, I want to be honest with myself. I really don't like practicing medicine." I knew I loved the creative aspect of writing from my yearbook experience. I would say, if you really want to make a move, do it early. Don't wait. A lot of doctors are so unhappy, because they get themselves locked into big financial obligations or rewards, and then they can't afford to change careers.

> "Don't get hung up on the money part of it. Get your foot in the door, doing something you really love doing, and eventually the money will come."

I knew one doctor who was totally bored. He was a friend of mine, an ophthalmologist in a small town in West Virginia. He hated it and was totally bored and lonely, but he was making $400,000 a year. If he went to a big city his salary would be cut in half. He got so trapped in making good money, that for fifteen years of his life he was literally miserable.

CEO AND CO-FOUNDER

6

Not everything is about money. I would say if you really think you are not going to like something, then make the move early. I have never looked back and I have loved every second of it. That has been a great stroke of luck for me. If you can have a job that you like going to everyday and you can't wait to get there, that's a gift.

Q. Can we squeeze a top five list out of you for people making the transition?

A. Make the transition earlier rather than later. Ask yourself, "What do you really like to do?" Then search out positions. You should try to find a position where you can utilize your degree. I still use my degree. In medical education I help thousands of patients by educating their doctors. You can always rationalize your choices, but leverage your degree. Don't abandon it. There is plenty out there. The medical degree (MD), which I call the "Mad Dog," does open up doors in all areas of life. It helps you get interviews.

Some other things: don't get hung up on the money part of it. Get your foot in the door, doing something you really love doing, and eventually the money will come. I met a surgeon who was 61 years old and very depressed. He said, "I don't like it anymore. I want to find something else. What is the best way to get into industry?" I said, "Offer to come in for no salary, almost like a senior internship. Just go in and advise and learn about the business side of it. Get that on your resume. You get that experience and become a success. Then you start commanding big money. No one is going to hire you without any experience on the business side at your age. Go in first for nothing. Prove yourself. Then you can start marketing yourself."

Q. Do you have any projects that you are working on for the future?

A. The biggest project is that we are re-launching "TheDoctorsChannel.com." We totally revamped it to make it even

7

more user-friendly. We are adding a huge CME component. We partnered with major publishers and we're going to expand and reach out internationally with the concept of continuing medical education presented in short five to seven minute videos, where doctors can get a quarter of a credit. With the concept of online, on demand, short, to-the-point videos of information doctors need to know now. That is the hottest thing. Of course, there will be a mobile app and an app for the iPad.

Q. So you're continuing with the discovery you made about our short attention spans? Is that a major contribution to the industry?

A. I think it's got everybody thinking. No longer can we put on hour-long webinars, and expect people to pay attention. We are also partnering with Reuters Health. Everyday we do a Reuters Health Doctor's Channel newscast where in two to three minutes we provide the world's hottest stories in medicine. Shot in a short, high-def video format, we provide the three top stories. Whether it is the lead article in Lancet or another journal, or something that made the news, it's always covered by us in short video format.

Q. Can you offer any personal slogans for success?

A. I always say, "Stay on the edge, more happens there." It's funny how people can stay so conservative. I once met a doctor from a pharmaceutical company who said, "I like to hire older physicians because they are not so cutting-edge. They are safe." I, of course, feel the opposite. It doesn't matter their age. I like to be around people who are constantly learning and willing to take a risk. That is how technology advances.

I've always been a proponent of colleague-to-colleague information transfer. It's so much more powerful. When it comes to medicine, doctors will say, "I'm in the doctors' lounge and another surgeon mentions an antibiotic he's using that got a

good result. That is very strong for me. That is important."
The colleague-to-colleague approach is always really powerful. That's the same for social media. By the way, on "The
Doctor's Channel" we have a Doc Life section where we recommend restaurants, sightseeing, theater, etc., in conven-
tion cities. Recommendations are so much more credible
when they come from a colleague.

Q. Is there anything else you would like to say before we sign off?

A. I didn't mention the power of the internet. I made my dog a
Bark-Mitzvah for his 13th birthday in dog years. We put it up
on "The Doctor's Channel" and the next thing you know CBS
saw it and we were on a reality series called "Greatest American Dog" two summers ago. It was amazing when people
recognized me on the street. Again, that is the power of the
internet. You put a video up and the next thing you know,
you're on network television.

The other part we didn't talk about is the balance of life. It
is not all work, it is not all medicine. You still have to have
hobbies and have time for doing that.

David's Best Transition Gems:
- You have to continually reinvent yourself.
- If you really want to make a move---don't wait! Do it early.
- Do what you really want to do.
- Never be hung up on the money part of it. First get your foot in the door, and eventually the money will come
- Don't give up your MD degree.

Communication Nuggets:
- Nobody has an attention span of more than 1-2 minutes any-more.
- In an age of media snacking, everybody gets their informa-tion in fragments throughout the day.
- Our whole concept was: Why not deliver information in 1-2

DR. DAVID BEST

minutes that get right to the point.
- 114 seconds is the optimal time for a video for regular people and probably the third of that for physicians.
- Editing is good manners.
- Doctors watch more online videos than the average consumer, because it is a quick way to access Continuing Medical Education (CME).

CEO AND CO-FOUNDER

"Being a physician executive is certainly a very viable career for a physician. It is not a career choice you can make coming right out of med school. You certainly have to have the clinical credibility of practicing medicine for a period of time to differentiate yourself from any other type of executive."

Dr. Mark Browne, Physician Executive

Dr. Mark Browne has ten years of physician executive experience and expertise and has performed a multitude of projects for small and large physician groups as well as health systems related to physician employment and compensation models, quality matters, implementation of contemporary practices, disruptive physician issues, fair market value analysis, development of clinical coding and reimbursement strategies, and hospital operations.

Dr. Browne is a national speaker on topics such as quality and healthcare reform with a focus on preparing for a value based model of healthcare delivery.

Dr. Browne is clinically trained as a primary care physician in both internal medicine and pediatrics, obtained his Doctorate of Medicine from Wright State University School of Medicine and holds a Masters of Medical Management from Carnegie Mellon University and has recently been named a Fellow in the American College of Physician Executives.

Q. When did you graduate from medical school?

A. I graduated from medical school in 1991 from Wright State University.

Q. What did you do after that? Did you go into a residency?

A. Yes, I did a combined residency in internal medicine and pediatrics.

Q. How did you enjoy that lifestyle?

A. I actually loved it. I had a great practice. After completing my residency, I joined a med-pediatric practice. We had a specialty practice in primary care where we took care of patients who didn't have anywhere else to go. We helped adolescents, former preemies with congenital heart disease. Many of our patients didn't have homes. They were adults suffering with pediatric diseases. It was an excellent practice.

Q. Why aren't you doing that now?

A. I was practicing in Dayton, Ohio, with a group called Miami Valley Hospital Enterprises, which grew from about 50 physicians in a multi-specialty employment group into about 200 physicians in six months. At the time, they were growing so rapidly and looking for physicians to get involved in creating governing structure. They were looking for as many specialties as they could find. I had interest and represented two specialties. So, they asked me to be a part of developing their governing structures. I ultimately got involved in the governance development, but also crafted compensation plans that weren't in existence at that point, just because their growth rate was so rapid. Even way back then we were looking at electronic records. It took us twenty years to get there.

I had a genuine interest, but at the same time I was rounding at three hospitals. I was still seeing 30-40 patients a day. And, to tell my wife's side of the story, I was working 115% of the time and doing administration the other 80%. I came home one night at about 7:30, which was par for the course after rounding at a couple hospitals, and my middle son had set the table for dinner, but hadn't set a place me. He said, "Because Dad never comes home." True story. I had to make a decision. Luckily, time and circumstance were both on my side.

I had befriended several of the administrators in the Miami Valley Hospital Enterprises structure. We had a gentleman's agreement that if one of the gentlemen ever left, I would be hired as a medical director. He went to Miami Valley and Middletown, which is now Atrium Medical Center, and took me along about three months later. I joined him as medical director of the primary care network down there.

Q. So your transition was an inside job?

A. Yes, it was. I had connections. Tim is a healthcare attorney. He left and took a job as the CEO of the primary care network. I was the Chief Medical Officer. After a year and a half he left and went back into full-time health law, both for professional and personal reasons. I took over as CEO of that network and was functionally the VPMA. They didn't have a VPMA. As a matter of fact the first VPMA starts tomorrow. It happens to be a friend of mine who I knew as an executive when I was there ten years ago.

Q. Are you presently in that position or have you evolved?

A. No, I have continued to evolve. Since that time I spent about eleven years in various Chief Medical Officer positions throughout the country. The position in Middletown was not evolving into a VPMA position. I went to the CEO and asked him if it was ever going to happen and he said, "Probably not right away." So I left. I took a senior VPMA position in Jackson, Michigan with Foote Hospital, which is now Allegiant Health. I was there for almost four years and then left that organization and went to Trover Regional Medicinal Center over in western Kentucky, which is where I met the company I'm with now, Pershing, Yoakley and Associates. We had a working relationship. I approached them and talked about some consulting opportunities. We checked each other out for a couple of months. I did some onsite work with them in some consulting roles and now I'm working with them full-time as a healthcare consultant with Pershing, Yoakley and Associates located in Knoxville. I've been there about two years. It's been a lot of fun.

Q. Congratulations. You probably still have your eyes open for other opportunities?

A. Absolutely.

Q. What were your biggest obstacles along the way?

A. If I had to choose it would be maintaining balance between work and home. In my eleven years or so in the CMO role I have had three jobs, so we have moved pretty frequently. I've got three boys who are now 13, 15, and 17. My oldest is graduating high school.

Q. What does the market look like for physician executives?

A. It is a wide open market around healthcare reform, particularly for experienced physician executives. There are many more physicians than there are experienced physician executives right now on the market. There are a certain number of physicians who are looking to get into the physician executive ranks and those physicians may have a little bit tougher time of it. But even so, there are a number of entry level and mid-level positions.

As an example, I've recently been working with an organization where they had one physician executive for fifteen hospitals. I had them move from one physician executive to six over the course of about eighteen months. Now they have two in place and are recruiting for four others. Obviously a larger system, but still the need is great.

Q. Is there anything else you would like to say?

A. Although it may be somewhat of a unique career choice, being a physician executive is certainly a very viable career for a physician. It is not a career choice you can make coming right out of med school. You certainly have to have the clinical credibility of practicing medicine for a period of time to differentiate yourself from any other type of executive. There are great MD/MBA programs out there right now which are giving good executive education to physicians. But it is very difficult, if not impossible to come out into a CMA or VPMA role without having first been in the trenches and seen patients.

A physician executive is a different type of creature in that you need to be able to speak both languages. You can be the translator between the medical staff or physicians in any setting, and other administrators. That's what really makes you unique. I didn't plan to become a physician executive, but I have absolutely no regrets. I would do it all over again the exact same way if I knew then what I know now. Especially being a health care consultant in the time of healthcare reform and redesign, it's a pretty good place for a physician executive to be.

Dr. Mark Browne

"Our calling is the point at which our deepest gladness meets the world's deepest need."

- Frederick Buechner

"I think the initial transition was the hardest. The real change is the realization, 'You know what? This is not the path for me.' You run into lots of external resistance. I know I had people tell me I was wasting my degree. Even worse, some told me I took up space in medical school that should have gone to someone else. I thought that was ridiculous. This is a degree that you earn. If you earn the degree, then you have the right to use it anyway you choose."

Dr. Jonathan Cargan, President, Freelance Author, Consultant

Jonathan Cargan, MD is President of Phoenix Ascendant Consulting, LLC, in Norristown, PA. Dr. Cargan has had extensive experience as a consultant and freelance writer for major pharmaceutical and vaccine companies. He has a current specialization in medical aspects of product promotion (phase IV) and strategic and competitive issues. He has consulted to three separate billion-dollar product franchises. He has functioned as a contract writer for several medical journal articles and writes updates in Infectious Disease for Websites supporting two major textbooks in this area.

Q. What drove you to medicine? Why did you originally want to take care of sick people?

A. To me, medicine was applied science. I just found the skills to be of interest to me. I got a better sense of my interest in the biological sciences in college. Then medicine seemed like a natural extension of that.

Q. What specialty did you choose?

A. My original goal was pediatric surgery, but I was training in general surgery by the time I made the decision to switch to a non-clinical career.

Q. How did you make that decision?

A. I would say about the second year of medical school, I started to have some inkling that maybe clinical practice was not for me. I was interested in the possibility of somehow combining medicine and business. I went through the usual clinical rotations as a med student, and then made the decision that I was going to use my internship as a litmus test. I was either going into clinical practice or not. Perhaps that was a bit of an overreaction with a general surgery internship. What area do you work in?

Q. I did my residency in emergency medicine.

A. Well, then you probably know that general surgery internships tend to be pretty harrowing. My experience was no different. I was in a fairly high powered program. It was good in a way that I got thrown in the deep end right away. That helped me make my decision that I really loved the operating room and doing surgery. However, I wasn't quite as enamored with other parts of it. I didn't feel I was getting out of it what I wanted, and I also felt my patients were not well-served by the training system. So, about one quarter of the way through my intern year, I said, "Okay, I have my answer." Then I finished out my internship.

I guess I went about it backwards. I left clinical practice first

PRESIDENT, FREELANCE WRITER, CONSULTANT

then started looking at my other options. I wouldn't recommend that as the best approach. There is a lot of uncertainty in it, but it turned out well for me, so I have no complaints. Definitely, I would now recommend looking before you leap and think about what you are going to do next. I completed my internship, looked for a couple of months, and then ended up in clinical research and development in the pharmaceutical industry.

Q. Did you enjoy that work?
A. I did. It's a very different perspective. In a way you go from taking care of an individual patient to running trials that involve thousands of patients. You are on the other end of things. You are dealing with agents that are just in the process of being characterized. You help to see what the efficacy and safety profile is going to look like, how it's going to be used in clinical practice, and what indications it will be good for. I think it is fascinating work. I stayed in R&D for four years. I got a good grounding in it.

Q. Are you still involved in that type of work?
A. I actually took another detour in my career. I always had a career aspiration to become a novelist. I quit my job in R&D and lived off my savings for two years in order to write my first novel. It was a lot of fun. I learned a lot, including the fact that first time writers should not quit their day job until they are published and selling well.

I decided to come back into the pharmaceutical industry on the market support side, an area called phase IV. After a drug or vaccine is approved, and is being marketed, I support further development of the drug marketing by making certain that all of the advertising is accurate, that it is communicating important and accurate information to clinicians and, in some cases, consumers. I've been working in that area since I came back as a consultant 14 years ago.

DR. JONATHAN CARGAN

19

Q. Are you still doing some creative writing on your own?

A. Absolutely, the novel is in rewrites now. I still hope to get it published. I already have ideas for other novels and other types of writing. That definitely is still on the agenda. Consulting gives me the time and energy to develop my writing.

Q. What were your biggest obstacles or breakthroughs while making the switch?

A. I think the initial transition was the hardest. You go through medical school and internship with the expectation that you are going to practice clinical medicine. That's why you are there. The real change is the realization, "You know what? This is not the path for me." You run into lots of external resistance. I know I had people tell me I was wasting my degree. Even worse, some told me I took up space in medical school that should have gone to someone else. I thought that was ridiculous. This is a degree that you earn. If you earn the degree, then you have the right to use it anyway you choose.

That was my initial obstacle, and I have to tell you, I feared being ostracized once I announced that I wasn't going to stay in surgery. But I had people with as many as nine years post-medical school training come to me and say they wished they could get out of clinical medicine too.

It can be a tough transition, and it's tough for a number of reasons including your own expectations of what your career could be. I think you have to make that decision carefully and give it some serious thought before you make the change. But after you escape those expectations, the sky is the limit. You really have so many possibilities open to you. I think the hard thing is when you go into clinical medicine with the expectation that you are going to stay there forever. Then your transition can take some courage.

PRESIDENT, FREELANCE WRITER, CONSULTANT

Q. Did you use a mentor or coach or any formal courses at all?

A. Not really. I made the initial transition about twenty years ago. There were physicians already working in the pharmaceutical industry and there always have been. There are conferences now where you can go to learn about non-clinical careers. There are people who are out there offering to coach you out of a clinical career. That really didn't exist back when I transitioned. That's why it took a couple of months for me to find another career path, which turned out to be pharmaceutical R&D. I'm really happy to see that there are many more resources now for physicians who want to pursue the non-clinical route. That wasn't very common back when I made my switch.

Q. You were a pioneer in the field.

A. To a certain extent. Like I said, there were other physicians in the pharmaceutical industry. I was not so much a pioneer for doing that. But it was much harder to find other career paths at that time. Now there are many more resources open to physicians so that they can learn about what their choices are.

Q. By going to a SEAK conference (www.SEAK.com: leaders in non-clinical physician education) or going online, it's amazing what's available now.

A. I have to tell you I'm really happy to see it. I think that is because clinical practice is worse now than it was twenty years ago. It is a much more hostile environment for so many reasons. I don't blame anyone who wants to get out of clinical practice, given what they are dealing with now.

Q. So, a writer. What a nice transition. You are definitely not stuck in some corporate jungle wondering what's next.

A. Well, no. We all have choices. I tend to really like autonomy, but it comes down to personality, what type of environment you want to work in. If you want to go to a large corporation

DR. JONATHAN CARGAN

21

and you are happy working in that environment, that is an option that is open to you. If you want to go to a smaller organization you can do that. If you want to work on your own, you can do that. Again, I think it's a lot about having choices, not only about what you do, but what kind of environment you chose to work in.

Q. Anything else you would like to add, or advice for others hoping to transition into non-clinical work?

A. I've met some really good people at SEAK conferences. I presented a talk there last year, and I will be back as faculty this year. I had an opportunity to meet a number of folks. There are very good people and resources out there. I like the old saying, "Physician, heal thyself." But I would add, "Physician, know thyself."

You really need to sit back and think about who you are, what your skills are, and what you would like to be doing. You need to become very clear about what your purpose and goal is and your vision for your career outside of clinical medicine, because this is not a transition to be taken lightly. Particularly if you have a family to support, you want to be very careful that you know where you are going before you take the leap. I think I've been very fortunate because I made a few decisions where I probably should have done more research, but things turned out OK anyway.

When I'm talking to someone who is contemplating switching careers, I advise them to first fully understand where they are coming from and what they want to achieve. They need to do plenty of research on what is out there that they might want to get involved in. I think people with medical degrees think they can do anything. Clearly those who go into clinical medicine are smart people and very capable, but this degree does not confer the ability to do any job. It's important to remember that.

PRESIDENT, FREELANCE WRITER, CONSULTANT

If you want a job in a certain industry or company, you are going to have to have the skill set and knowledge base they are looking for. The MD may be helpful. There is a bit of a halo effect. It does buy you some instant credibility. The problem is that once you get down to the details, you still have to be able to do the specific job you applied for. I think it is important to remember that the MD is not a kind of jack-of-all-trades kind of thing. You really have to think about where you are headed and get yourself as qualified as possible for the work you want to do.

Q. I've heard that before. It's nice to have an MD, but you have to be able to do the job. You are part of their team now, not the captain.

A. Right. There are situations where you will be called upon to be the captain of the team and then you need good leadership skills. As an MD at the hospital you are given a lot of instant leadership credibility, but when you get out in a major corporation or consulting firm, you need to know how to lead. Those people won't necessarily follow you instantly. You are going to need a little different skill set than in a hospital, or in a practice setting where you own the practice.

Q. You said you had a few more things you wanted to add?

A. A part of my practice is freelance writing. I know many freelance medical writers who have nothing more than a bachelor's degree, no Ph.D. or MD, but they are absolutely outstanding writers. They are quite knowledgeable, they know the literature and are excellent writers. They can write a masterful paper on any medical subject. They often share with me the silly assumption some physicians make, that because we have an MD, we think we are automatically good writers. This goes back to making sure your skills are in place. If you have never had any formal training in writing and you want to write, I would at a minimum go and get an honest assessment of your skills. You may very well need to take some training in writing to make sure that you are a capable writer. The MD does not guarantee that.

Q. I couldn't agree with you more. I started my transition last year to become a fulltime writer. This book literally fell into my lap. I realized that I was going to have to get some training along the way.

A. Have you looked at the American Medical Writers Association? It's at AMWA.org. They run courses and you can get certification through them. They run courses for basic writing skills like grammar and punctuation and all that basic stuff from grade school. I would recommend this organization for specific training and certification.

Q. Anything else you would like to add? Do you have any slogans or guiding principles that have gotten you through your transition or tough times?

A. Sure, I would say if you want to run your own business, you have to think like a business person. Again, you might have some new skills to learn. You have to remember that your client is king. It's a new experience for a lot of physicians, a very different relationship from that we have with our patients. Now you need to treat your client differently. If you commit to a deadline, then you have to keep it. You have to have good business practices. There are many other issues involved in running a business that you will have to keep your eyes on. You may have pushed these skills off on your office manager before, but now you are going to have to either take them on yourself, or hire someone to help you with them. It is a different environment than most MDs are used to operating in.

I would also like to caution you about going into the pharmaceutical industry at the moment. I know that a lot of physicians look at that as a natural place to go. It actually is. It's a really good place. They appreciate your clinical knowledge and experience. But, this industry has been under attack for a number of years now. In particular, the relationship between physician consultants and companies is under a lot of scrutiny right now. So, what I would suggest is if you are thinking of moving over to work in pharma, don't count on that industry entirely. I don't know where the industry is going at the moment, so I would look at maybe having a pharma component, but not necessarily depend on them completely for employment.

The other thing is, there are other areas of medical writing besides writing papers or doing work for pharmaceutical companies. There's consumer writing and other types. Working on your core writing skills can only help open doors in terms of the many choices available to you.

Dr. Jonathan Cargan

"Every new day begins with possibilities. It's up to us to fill it with the things that move us towards progress and peace."

- Ronald Reagan

"There's a generational change we are going through right now as a world and a society. We have to teach ourselves a different way because all of our previous role models – our parents, our teachers, everybody around us – believed that you do one thing, you do it for life, and then you retire, get sick and die. But that's not the same world view that I have anymore. Mine is that we all have creative power."

Dr. Lisa Chu , Musician, Life Coach, Entrepreneur

Dr. Lisa Chu, M.D., musician, former physician, life coach, entrepreneur, & founder of The Music Within Us, provides support, encouragement, and guidance for adults seeking a more creative approach to life, greater courage to live with passion, and an overall sense of joy and freedom. She has an A.B. with honors in Biochemical Sciences from Harvard University, and an M.D. from the University of Michigan Medical School.

Q. Why did you go to medical school? What were you hoping to find?

A. I went to med school because it was expected of me. In my family that was the level of education that was expected. My brother is a doctor, so to me it felt doable. Even though it was never my heart's desire, I could see the value of doing it, intellectually.

Q. When did you decide that you wanted to leave medicine? What came over you?

A. The moment came in January of my third year of medical school. I was on a vascular surgery rotation. I knew the whole time that I didn't love medicine. Just seeing all the residents around me, and how they looked like the walking dead. So I wondered, "These people must feel some passion. It must be their love or perhaps they were been born to do this. Why else would they be willing to put up with this kind of stress?"

When I finally spoke to a few of them, I found they had come into it for the same reasons as me. It was fine. It was something to do. Then in vascular surgery I saw a few vignettes that really brought it home for me. I saw two out of five residents on my team working even though they were ill themselves. They would be performing an operation, and would have to leave the OR to throw up in the scrub sink. Then they'd come right back to surgery. I looked at that and wondered, "At what point do we say, is this the right choice for me? Or is this something I am doing because I feel I have no other choices?"

The epiphany for me was the day I realized that if I really didn't want to, I didn't have to do a residency. I verbalized that on the phone to my brother. I said, "You know what? I don't have to do a residency," because I was feeling very limited by my choice of specialties, and I couldn't imagine myself in any of them. And he said, "Yeah, you are right. If you don't want to, you shouldn't." That was a moment of liberation for me.

From then on, when I finally freed myself of the idea that I had to become a doctor, I began to see so many other options. I guess you could call it luck, but I finally felt open to consider all of my possibilities.

Q. What was the next step you took?

A. Around that time, McKenzie began recruiting doctors and Ph.D.'s for their work in firms as consultants. So I went and interviewed for that program and got in. I was able to experience a weekend of what consulting might be like. It turned out I wasn't interested in that particular firm, but it opened my eyes to my other possibilities and it was good for me to see real people who had made this choice. I think it was very important for me to see other people who had gone through the whole program, gotten their degrees, and then decided to go in a different direction. And they seemed to be doing just fine.

That was in 2000, so the whole .com thing was going on. I became interested in that area, but I had no idea what a venture capitalist was. I had friend who was one, and through the McKenzie process I started talking to a lot of people about new ideas.

Q. Did you use a mentor or a coach or any of the online services?

A. No, at that time I had no clue about any of that. I went right from college to medical school and knew very little about what my other options were.

Q. Would you tell me about your first job after medical school? Did you actually get paid?

A. Yes, it was in venture capital. My first step was calling a local venture capitalist. He ended up offering me an internship which I did during medical school. Then when I graduated from medical school without a job, I joined a venture capital firm. I worked for free for six weeks, and then they hired me. I just wanted to do the work.

Q. So you got a job, but did you have some respect? Or were you are still exploring at this point or looking for something different?

A. Actually, I was with that firm for three and a half years. I became a partner and realized I had respect and status, but that life was more about what I could do, not about what I wanted to do. It has been a long learning process for me, because up until that point it was still about doing what everyone else told me to do.

Six years ago I left that job and moved across the country to California, where I always wanted to live. I started my own violin school, my dream since age four. I grew that violin school for five and half years. But as of this January, I transitioned out of that. Now I'm a life coach.

I have been training as a life coach since last year. I am at the beginning of something new again, and life continues to unfold for me. This is my own approach to life, my own philosophy that joy and freedom come from living in a place of creativity. I am just learning this on my own and I have many mentors and coaches in the community for support. That's my personal take on life.

I think there's a generational change we are going through right now as a world and a society. Right now we have to teach ourselves a different way because all of our previous role models – our parents, our teachers, everybody around us – believed that you do one thing, you do it for life, and then you retire, get sick and die. But that's not the same world view that I have anymore. Mine is that we all have creative power.

Q. How is the life coach business? Let's say another doctor would like to become a coach, what is involved in that job? Do you need extra training?

A. Right now it's a pretty new field. Anyone can decide they

MUSICIAN, LIFE COACH, ENTREPRENEUR

are a life coach. I personally went through training. There are many different training programs. It's not a regulated profession. I did receive training in a year long program, but I would recommend doing whatever you feel comfortable doing, and if training is part of that, then that's what you need to do.

Q. So you left your violin school? That had to be tough from the creativity point of view.

A. I started out from scratch and I grew it, and it became successful. But I was learning more and more about creativity. I was trained as a classical violinist and I was training these kids. I like to say I used to train three year olds to be more like grownups, but now I teach adults to be more like three year olds.

Q. What was your biggest obstacle going from medical school to becoming a life coach?

A. The fear of disappointing other people. At every stage I have had to leave some things behind to grow more – that's the biggest obstacle.

Q. Can you offer any tips or advice for others who are in a transition and might be experiencing the same things?

A. To recognize that the idea that you are disappointing other people, or any other obstacle you feel you are facing when you transition, is just a thought. Our mental thought patterns are habitual and unconscious to us, and yet they can cause all of our suffering, including feelings of being trapped or fear – all of it. When you first recognize that, you learn to observe your own thoughts, and play with them, developing what I call "yoga of the mind." You learn flexibility, balance and strength in your own mind. The obstacles that you think you are facing are not real, they are only things that exist in your own mind.

Q. What are your plans for future projects?

A. I am working on a book as well as a CD of improvised, original violin music. I am also building my speaking career. I would like to speak to groups of people who are experiencing burn-out or are at risk for burnout, college seniors or medical students, or adults who are in transition and are finally ready to commit to a conscious life, in line with their passion.

I think the world will be changed by people living from a place of passion. We've been afraid of it for a couple generations, but it's time now. We need creativity. We need new ways of thinking that will help us shape our world for the better. I believe it begins on an individual level. That is my approach. There are plenty of systemic problems to solve, but it starts with each individual looking at their own thinking. There's a lot of finger pointing and blame going on right now. I would like to teach people how to bring it inside and become gentler and more compassionate within themselves, so they can bring that back into the world.

MUSICIAN, LIFE COACH, ENTREPRENEUR

5

"It's never too late to change what you want to be when you grow up."
Dr. Kenneth Cohn, Author, Founder, Cancer Survivor

Dr. Cohn describes himself as a recovering academic surgeon. He obtained his M.D. degree from Columbia College of Physicians and did his residency at the Harvard-Deaconess Surgical Service. He was Assistant Professor of Surgery at SUNY Health Science Center at Brooklyn and moved to Dartmouth-Hitchcock Medical Center as Associate Professor of Surgery and Chief of Surgical Oncology at the VA Hospital at White River Junction. With the change in the medical economic climate, Dr. Cohn entered the MBA program of the Tuck School at Dartmouth and graduated June 1998.

He worked initially as a consultant at Health Advances, assisting 6 firms to commercialize new products. After joining the Cambridge Management Group in 1999, he led change-man-

DR. KENNETH COHN

agement initiatives for physicians at affiliated hospitals within the Yale New Haven, Banner Colorado, Cottage Santa Barbara, and Sutter Sacramento Health Systems.

Dr. Cohn founded HealthcareCollaboration.com in 2006 to create services and information products for healthcare leaders that would help them engage physicians to improve care for their communities.

He founded TheDoctorpreneur.com in 2009 to help aspiring physician entrepreneurs learn business skills not taught in medical school, residency, or fellowship training. Dr. Cohn's writing experience includes over 45 published articles in peer-reviewed healthcare journals. His article, *The Tectonic Plates Are Shifting: Cultural Change vs. Mural Dyslexia*, won the Dean Conley Award in 2009 from the American College of Healthcare Executives for the best article in a healthcare management publication.

He has written two books, <u>Better Communication for Better Care: Mastering Physician-Administration Collaboration</u>, and <u>Collaborate for Success! Breakthrough Strategies for Engaging Physicians, Nurses, and Hospital Executives</u>, published by Health Administration Press, 2005 and 2006. Dr. Cohn is the editor of <u>The Business of Healthcare</u>, a three-volume set, published 2008 that comprises physician practice management, leading healthcare organizations, and improving systems of care.

Dr. Kenneth Cohn, MD, MBA, FACS, is a practicing surgeon and cancer survivor who divides his time between; Providing locum tenens general surgical coverage in ME, NH, and VT, helping doctors and hospital administrators work together, and guiding fellow physicians who want to work smarter rather than harder.

Q. Could you tell me a little bit about your upbringing?
A. I grew up in Buffalo, New York. My father was a neurosurgeon who practiced for 25 years as a solo practitioner. I got to see what life was like for a physician both through my father's experience, and by growing up in a physician's family.

AUTHOR, FOUNDER, CANCER SURVIVOR

Q. When did you decide to become a physician yourself?

A. I made the decision to go to medical school, but it wasn't until I got through my fourth year of med school, that I became clear about what I wanted to do.

Q. How did that appear to you? Where did it come from?

A. I was in a conversation with the head of the Smithers Institute. She said to me, "So why are you going into surgery?" I told her that for the longest time I thought I would wind up in medicine or OB/GYN, because I thought I needed to do something different from my father. Once I got into an environment with general surgeons, I realized there are a lot of different personalities. I found my path. I kept a journal all through medical school. That was the only entry I ever titled: "Turning the Corner."

Q. Excellent. Did you enjoy being a general surgeon? Did you feel fulfilled?

A. Yes, I felt fulfilled, and I still do. My practice now covers surgical practices in Maine, New Hampshire, and Vermont. I provide relief to physicians who otherwise wouldn't have a chance to have many weekends off or spend a two-week vacation with their family.

Q. What made you turn towards the non-clinical aspect of your career?

A. I think we're all a product of the events that hit us. In 1996, the VA hospital where I was working announced a budget crisis. They fired five of us part-time physicians and surgeons. We were told we had no rights and had to look for other jobs. Because it happened on Valentine's Day, we called it the "Val-

> "My income actually went down by about half once I got my MBA and began working as an associate in a consulting company."

Dr. Kenneth Cohn

entine's Day Massacre."

Within two weeks I had offers from New Mexico and New Jersey. I said to my wife, "See, things are working out. Which one should I look at first?" When she broke down in tears and said, "I'm not ready to move. I've been here four years and people are just starting to pay attention to me," I realized that I needed to do something different. So, I applied to the graduate business program at the Tuck School at Dartmouth. In December 1995, an article in USA Today identified only 75 physicians with an MBA degree. I was a pioneer.

Surgery is a good practice for this transition. You become comfortable making major decisions based on limited information. You can never really get perfect information in patient care, and yet we expect that when we embark on a career choice.

The second thing that helped from my background as a surgeon was that we have situations where patients don't do as well as we

> **"I think that we all can benefit from coaches who help us see our blind spots."**

would like. If we are going to continue doing surgery, we need to accept these circumstances as learning experiences.

Q. What advice would you give in making decisions for those who are not general surgeons?

A. I think that people need to become more comfortable with their intuitive side. Most of us males deny that we have such a thing as feelings, although we talk about things like surgical intuition and medical intuition. As my wife says, it comes from trusting your gut.

If you think about it, what happens with a lot of physicians is that we have a pretty well-prescribed career path from kindergarten through high school, college, medical school, and residency. We know where we are going, either practice or academics. Once we go beyond that, we start looking at alternatives. If there is no clear path, we have to create one ourselves.

A lot of times, we view learning as failure. It's not failure at all. It's just that we have a certain concept of the universe, which we test it out, and find there is more to learn. Learning is something we tend to be impatient with, especially those of us who chose surgery.

Q. How about the transition into your career? How would you describe it? You have many roles as the CEO of your company TheDoctorpreneur.com. How was your cash flow and income affected during your transition time?

A. One thing I needed to realize was that having another degree didn't mean I was going to get paid more. My income actually went down by about half once I got my MBA and began working as an associate in a consulting company. I understood why. Right after graduating from medical school, I wasn't worth as much as I was after five years of surgical residency. But, it was tough for my wife to understand why my salary dropped by 50% after I completed a two-year MBA degree

Q. How about now? How is your income compared to your previous salary as a surgeon?

A. I think that the recession has made all of our lives less predictable. I became part of an executive coaching program this year, because last year my income went up 15% over the previous year, due to only two clients. I recognized that I couldn't have a situation where all of my income was dependent on one or two clients. The coach told me that I needed to do a better job of positioning my skills as a vital investment that improved physicians' and hospitals' performance, rather than a discretionary expense. I think that we all can benefit from coaches who help us see our blind spots.

Q. What were your biggest obstacles during your period of transition?

A. I'm still in transition. I have a sign in my office that says, "It's never too late to change what you want to be when you grow up."

One of the breakthroughs that a friend helped me see was the concept of a frontier. What she helped me recognize is that most of my work is relational. I have to look at this as a frontier. A lot of my work is about solving problems for my client, as well as building a long-term relationship. Learning to listen better is a lifelong journey.

Q. A focus of Physicians in Transition at the SEAK conference was specifically focused on that jump, maybe it's more like a leap...

A. From clinical to non-clinical is a leap, there's no doubt about it.

Q. If you hadn't decided to become a doctor, what other careers were you considering?

A. I grew up during the Vietnam War. I knew that, even if I wasn't willing to fight in the war, I was willing to treat the injured. Growing up under those circumstances helped condition me. I majored in sociology in college, mostly just to get away from the pre-med students. They were so cutthroat competitive. They represented the last thing I ever wanted to be. Certainly, they weren't the kind of people I wanted to get my healthcare from.

I entertained, briefly, the idea of staying in academics, but sociology didn't seem like anything I would enjoy doing for a long period of time. But I still use sociology today when I make up questionnaires. The concepts that I learned, like self-fulfilling prophecy, and that if we cannot agree, all the

AUTHOR, FOUNDER, CANCER SURVIVOR

laws of the land are insufficient, are concepts that I use all the time. It certainly was relevant from that standpoint.

Q. So you use your sociology training. I see you as a pioneer who solves day-to-day problems while establishing a thriving community in the cosmic entrepreneurial frontier.

A. I know doctors enjoy learning from fellow doctors. I've certainly learned from other doctors as well. Part of the process I use when I work with doctors is mentoring. I call it co-mentoring, because I feel as though I learn at least as much from them as they learn from me.

> "Just before the breakthrough is often when we feel on the verge of a breakdown."

Q. Do you have any favorite slogans, principles or mantras or guiding principles that you like to follow?

A. There are lots of them that change from week to week. One is Ronald Reagan's: "You showed me the manure, now show me the pony." I find myself challenged from time to time to see the gift in my challenges.

I believe that the concept of honoring the present moment is important. One of the things that we haven't talked about yet, is that I'm a cancer survivor. During residency, I developed lymphoma. Through that experience, I learned what it is like to be both a doctor and a patient.

My chemotherapy taught me to live in the present. T h e r e were a number of times when I was lying in bed, and if I just turned a little bit I would have to get up and vomit. Sometimes I vomited as many as a dozen times a day. So, that taught me to live in the present, and not be stuck in the past or future.

DR. KENNETH COHN

Q. On your website, TheDoctorpreneur.com, you have a fantastic knowledge base. I find it addictive to read. How did you arrive at that formula? What are the different roles you see yourself in as you provide this service to physicians?

A. Steve Babitsky was looking for a non-clinical physician a few years ago and I applied, but he chose somebody who was in Pharma rather than me. At that time Pharma was hiring. I decided that the only way I was going to be asked to teach this course was to take it as a student. He wrote to me before the course started, and asked me what were my three goals? I wrote back, "I only have one goal. I want to see what the unmet needs are and fill them. I want to tell you what I could do to teach the course in a way that might add value to your students." About one week after I sent him my synopsis, he told me he would like me to teach. That was last year, September 2009.

As I was preparing for the course, two clients cancelled due to recessionary pressures, and the phone stopped ringing. I had a chance to prepare for the course in a far more intense way than if I had been busy clinically or with consulting or speaking. That is when I decided to create the website, TheDoctorpreneur.com. I'm in a physicians mentoring group. We tested out a number of concepts as we tried to figure out what might appeal to fellow physician travelers. The idea of 'expand your universe' was something that resonated with everyone at the table. We all felt that we were in roles that were confining and that we could do so much more then we were actually doing.

Q. The idea of getting that degree and a specialty and then riding it straight through for 30 or 40 years, that doesn't exist in medicine anymore?

A. My father was at the same hospital from 1952 until he died in 1991. I don't know too many physicians now who are at the same hospital they started out at.

Q. The physicians that you see now are running away from medicine. Are they attracted to finding a new niche for themselves?

A. I believe so, as the following story shows: At the last SEAK conference I was doing mentoring every 15 minutes, almost like speed- dating. One man I met was a really glum-faced emergency doc. He could barely make eye contact with me. I asked him a few basic questions, mainly out of Jim Collins' Good to Great. I asked, "What are you really good at? What do you get paid for? What are the things that you feel passionate about?" He said, "I'm really good at cartooning." Then he asked, "How is this relevant to healthcare?"

I described to him one of my own experiences. In my residency, a busy head and neck surgeon, was trying to figure out how to give his patients the oral care that they needed after a major operation. His chief resident said, "There is no use writing anything down for the nurses aides. All they read are comic books." Then the attending surgeon thought, "That's a great idea!" He made a comic book on how to provide for his patients' oral care.

After I told the story, the glum-faced ER doc's eyes opened wide. He said, "I work in an emergency room with people from the inner city. We try to explain to them about bad staph infections and the need to wash their hands. You've given me a great idea!"

I saw him an hour later in the bathroom. He said, "I want you to know I am walking so much lighter now. I have so many ideas that I can't scribble them down fast enough." I had helped him reconnect with his passion in a way he hadn't done since medical school.

DR. KENNETH COHN

41

Q. Excellent. How about you? How do you want to be remembered? What do you want people to say about you after you are gone?

A. I said to my wife at dinner, "I want only three words on my tombstone." So she asked, "What are those?" I said, "He was trainable." She looked at me and said, "You better live a while longer."

I'm doing things now in my coaching program that I've never done before in my life. I made welcome videos for my website. I did some audio podcasts and recently a video podcast on YouTube, Making Sense of Healthcare Reform. I'm reaching out to physicians, nurses, and hospital leaders to build a Creative Collaboration group on LinkedIn. If it makes me initially uncomfortable, I go for it. That makes me feel like I am growing.

Q. It sounds like you're having fun with it. That's sort of like being a resident.

A. Enjoying the process and enjoying my family is certainly part of the fun. I think we all get impatient with the idea that we're on a journey. The only destination that I know is one where people say, "He's gone now." If we live our life well, we live on in our students' minds and in our families and friends.

I remember when I was an attending surgeon in a hospital in Vermont, one of the residents said, "Dr. Cohn, after working with you, I've started keeping file cards. I'm going to do my cases the way you do yours." We do not realize sometimes what our impact can be.

Q. So basically, if someone wants to get help from you, they have many paths just within your corporation?

A. I try to make it easy for people to interact with me in a variety of different ways. I use the concept of the funnel. If people want to read an article about getting over job frustrations, it's there for them on my TheDoctorpreneur.com website. If they want to know whether they are experiencing burnout, I've written a book chapter about that in my first book: Better Communication for Better Care. If they feel that change is a real thorn in their side and they want to be inspired by changes around the United States, they might read my book, Collaborate for Success. It has 13 chapters about changes that help people get in touch with what attracted them to careers in healthcare in the first place.

The blog posts and the articles that I write draw people in. I feel a little bit like Johnny Appleseed, planting seeds, and never knowing where the orchards will blossom. But I'm certain that they will blossom all over the country. I have worked in 40 states over the past decade and taught in China, Italy, England, and Sweden.

Q. So clients can contact you for regular mentoring or coaching?

A. Absolutely. I'm also happy to work with their hospital executives to solve physician-administrator communication problems. Recently, my coach asked me to devise a new service based on my unique gifts. So, I asked ten different CEOs that I worked with, "What is my unique gift?" They told me: "That's obvious. You have the ability to engage physicians, in all their ranting and raving. Crafting their ideas into a carefully thought-out action plans to improve their practice environment, not only for them but for their patients as well." Those are the things that I do to make peoples' lives easier and make their time count. As you know, when physicians feel as though their time isn't respected, they don't feel personally respected.

Q. You have a reasonable amount of showmanship too. Your video is very good, with the visuals, the pace and the content. On the phone too, you have a great presence.

A. You're very kind. That's my journey as well. When I first decided to do a video, I did the first one to keep me humble. I crashed and burned. The only negative comment I got about the last video on the website was from my daughter, whom I call my ideal co-mentor. She said, "Dad, you sound like a used car salesman."

We all have to get in touch with that side of ourselves where we apply the tools we have to help people succeed. I think that being willing to take that leap, as you called it earlier, involves summoning the courage to take a calculated, or what I call 'prudent' risk.

Q. Is there anything else you would like to add that we haven't touched on yet?

A. I think that the most important thing is for people to become comfortable with the idea that there are a lot of different things they can do. The greatest applause I got at the SEAK conference last year occurred when I made the comment about people saying to me, "But, you are wasting your clinical training." There are two words for that: "Bull shit!"

I think that we need to understand that we are multi-talented people who have a variety of different pathways to choose. Whatever path we chose, that is the right one for us. We just need to listen to other people and be comfortable with listening to our own internal voices. What is it that makes us excited about going on in our day-to-day life? I think that if you find a way to align what you do with your basic values and passion, then you won't feel like you're working. You won't mind working on weekends. I got up at 5:15 am to write an article before taking my wife out for Valentine's Day. It didn't feel like work. It felt like something that I wanted to do, because it was important to me.

Q. When you come to a decision through the use of intuition or passion, you then discover. Or, as some people say, the collision of intuition and intellect is an 'Ah-ha!' moment.

A. That's a good way of looking at it. Some of our 'ah-has' don't come immediately. Joseph Conrad talked about the night journey. I've had several night journeys over the last few years. Every so often, it is natural to wonder, "Why is this so difficult? Why do I feel like I'm climbing one false summit after another?" Just before the breakthrough is often when we feel on the verge of a breakdown. We need to recognize that we are all in this together and that we can help one other.

DR. KENNETH COHN

"It takes great courage for men and women to discover their calling. After all, it may not be what you are doing now, and to face your calling squarely may cause some significant disruption in your life."

- from the book Prioritize by Joe Calhoun and Bruce Jeffrey

6

"I chose this profession because I can do things that immediately make a difference in people's lives while contributing something to the art and science of surgery."

Dr. Jay Crutchfield, Surgical Arts

Dr. Crutchfield's proficiency in the surgical arts today is a reflection of his desire to excel in the profession. With his medical degree, followed by many years of training and board-certification requirements, he has the educational foundation necessary to deliver top-quality care to his patients. Some of his accomplishments include:

- Board-Certified: American Board of Surgery
- MD: Mt. Sinai School of Medicine of the City University of New York, NY
- BA: Magna Cum Laude, Chemistry, University of Arizona, Tucson, AZ
- Internship, Residency, Chief Residency: General Surgery, VA Hospital, Des Moines, IA
- General Surgery, Mercy Hospital & Medical Center, Des

Moines, IA
- Trauma Surgery, St. Joseph's Hospital & Medical Center, Phoenix, AZ
- Pediatric Surgery, University of Iowa Hospitals & Clinics, Iowa City, IA
- Fellow: American College of Surgeons
- Member: American Society for Parenteral & Enteral Nutrition, American Society of General Surgeons , Society of Laparoendoscopic Surgeons, American Society of Breast Surgeons, American Hernia Society
- Special Interests: Endoscopy, Laparoscopy & Adult General Surgery

Dr. Crutchfield was born and raised in Arizona and now lives here in Prescott. In his free time, he enjoys traveling, reading, collecting rock 'n' roll memorabilia (especially KISS collectibles), deep-sky astronomy and astrophotography.

Q. When did you graduate from medical school?
A. I graduated in 1989 and then entered a general surgery residency in Des Moines, Iowa for five years.

Q. Did you go into regular practice after that?
A. Interestingly, I couldn't find a job. Even though there were a lot of general surgery jobs all over the country, there were very few jobs available for those who weren't young doctors coming out to take on the call. I looked and looked, and finally found a job. It took me probably a year and a half after finishing my residency to find a job with a general surgeon who didn't want to use and abuse me. I was with him for about two years. That worked out well. It was a good experience.

I entered private practice in general surgery. It took me some time, and I worked in emergency rooms to pay the bills. Then I found that job in general surgery.

SURGICAL ARTS

Q. What changed to lead you to leave your clinical practice?

A. I just got a job about a month ago teaching medical students at a brand new osteopathic school in Mesa, Arizona. I am an M.D., but this is a non-clinical academic job. I have been looking for a non-clinical job for about two years, because of my increasing dissatisfaction with health care.

Q. Did you have a plan at all? Did you use any websites or mentors?

A. I did. I used several websites and actually found none of them helpful. I found the best way to find a job is almost always word of mouth – connections with people who know you. It really has worked out great. I used a website called Up Ladders and paid $189 and got absolutely zero results. It was of absolute no help.

Most of the applications today are done online and you would think that even an online rejection would be easier. But I didn't hear back from a single job I applied for. I never even got rejection letters. I just heard nothing.

Q. Were there any other tough parts in making the transition, such as financially?

A. Yes, in fact if I had stayed in my current profession as a general surgeon, within a year I would have probably been bankrupt. That's not because I've been sued or because I am a bad doctor. I have been in practice now for almost 16 years, but with the amount of overhead that it takes to run an office and what Medicare pays, and none payments, there is no way to make a living. People come to the emergency room and you never see them again. These are the kind of pressures that are pushing doctors to become employees in their hospitals just to stay alive. The public does not understand this. The public has no understanding of the job. We will always appear to be rich doctors to the public, and a lot of that is because the media does such a great job covering raising health insurance premiums with the implication that

DR. JAY CRUTCHFIELD

doctors are getting paid more. That couldn't be further from the truth.

So when I began to see my numbers fall – and my numbers have fallen for probably the past six or seven years in a row – I could see the writing on the wall. There came a point where I personally refused to work harder for less money, where I personally refused to book a full office and a full clinic in order to pay the bills. You can only work so hard for so much money before you burn out. And I saw this happening to me. I see it happening to my colleagues, but for a variety of reasons they choose to stay. They may feel like they have to stay, or they won't look hard enough to find a job outside.

Q. I know in medical school we were taught to just work beyond what you can do, especially in general surgery. I mean, that's the whole martyrdom, right?

A. That's an excellent comment. It is martyrdom to a point. It is. That is excellent insight into the profession.

My story is perhaps a little different. I am a native of Arizona, and I went to high school in a public high school. I went to college at the University of Arizona and I grew up basically dirt poor. You don't know you are poor when you are there. It's only when you look back on it that it becomes obvious. I finished college in 1985 and was not accepted to the University of Arizona med school. Even then, Arizona had a law on the books that said if an applicant to the state medical school is from rural Arizona and agrees to practice in rural Arizona when he graduates, he will be given special consideration for admission. Well, I didn't get in. And several of my friends who were quite qualified also didn't get in. I have been all over Arizona and I have always practiced in rural Arizona. So I did exactly what I promised them I would do, accept that my education would never be paid for by the state of Arizona.

But it really left me feeling bitter. Because of that I have always refused to accept what we call "access patients," which are Medicaid patients. My logic is simple. If I wasn't good enough to attend the state medical school and have part of my tuition paid for by state tax dollars, and it cost me close to $175,000 of my own money to go to private medical school, why should I come back to Arizona to take care of Arizona's indigent? It made no sense to me. So I take care of the indigent population through the emergency rooms, and I only take care of those patients that I choose to, on an elective basis.

So I could be busy – sure. I could open up my doors and I let in a flood of Medicaid patients, but I refuse to do that on principle.

Q. Perhaps you need a job with more respect, such as being a professor?

A. I don't know if that's necessarily true. I mean, I love surgery. I like what I do, but I don't like everything that has happened to our profession. I don't like seeing on television where a professional sports player, professional athlete, or a Hollywood star makes millions and millions of dollars, and yet people demand that their heart transplant be paid for by the government. While those operations are expensive, it seems to me that the profession has lost a great deal of respect. I don't want to be part of that. I don't want to be part of a profession where, when I see a patient in the emergency room, I accept all responsibility for that patient's visit.

Let me give you an example. If a patient comes into the emergency room and has a medical condition, I am covered by my malpractice insurance. I think the patient also needs to take more responsibility not only for his/her own health, whether they smoke or drink or shoot drugs, but I think every hospital in America should have a kiosk right out front

DR. JAY CRUTCHFIELD

where patients have to buy their own malpractice insurance, just like buying flight insurance when you get on an airplane. It has always irritated me that we don't get to choose our patients. We don't choose them, they choose us. Some are easy to take care of and some are very complex. But when the ER calls, we, the physicians involved, assume all of the liability, all of it. That has never made sense to me. I think just about every doctor in America would agree with me, but I feel the recent health care reform sent a very loud, clear message: our opinion doesn't count. There was no tort reform, there were no Medicare fixes, there were no SGR fixes. It's all the professional organization that we belong to that lobby to get these snafus fixed and none of them were addressed.

I can't take it anymore. I see it from a different perspective. I educated myself at a private medical school. After I finished my training program in Iowa, I came back to a small town in Arizona. I went to a local bank and said, "I would like to set up shop and be a general surgeon here in your town." The bank manager asked me how much money I owed. I said I owed about $175,000 in school loans, and he said, "Jay, we cannot give you a loan to start your practice. You hold too much debt." I looked at him and I said, "What am I supposed to do? I have skills, I have training, but I have school loan debt." He said, "I am sorry, but we consider you a high risk." So that town lost a general surgeon that day. I just said thank you and left. I kept looking for another town.

That was my experience after I finished my residency. Like I said, there were a lot of jobs where the young doctor took all the calls. When I finally found another general surgeon who owned his own equipment and had his own office, I helped pay overhead and pay rent. I have a different perspective on why there are so few doctors in rural Arizona. It's because they can't make a living there. Somebody has to pay the overhead.

So I am bitter. There's no doubt about it. I am angry. I'm upset. I think there are fixes to the health care system that could have made a lot of doctors happier across the country. I abhor the idea that a 90 year old lady can come to the emergency room, have most of her bill paid by society, and then can potentially turn around and sue the physicians taking care of her.

My argument is that any money won in a malpractice suit against a physician who was working on a patient who was using state or federal dollars, should go back in the government. If you let society pay your bill, then malpractice money should go back to fund the society's program.

Obviously others don't see it that way, so I have decided to make a change. I am 46 years old and I am in debt up to my ass. We are now forced to make payment on what's called a "tail" for our malpractice insurance. They say we will cover you, and then when you leave your practice, you have to trade your school loan debt of $175,000 for a tail of $175,000. It makes no sense. It's a treadmill of debt that never ends. It's a treadmill that I have to get off of!

Q. Are you now teaching medical students?
A. I am closing my practice down this month, and June first I take a job at an osteopathic medical school teaching gross anatomy.

Q. So that will clearly solve a lot of your problems?
A. I hope so, but I am not going to buy a tail. I don't have the money for it.

You know the public doesn't even know about the concept of

DR. JAY CRUTCHFIELD

the tail. The public doesn't even understand that the whole concept of the tail is what keeps so many doctors in practice. So many of the young docs simply can't walk away, because they know they have the price of a tail hanging over their head.

We had an obstetrician who had moved into our town about two years ago. She had to sell her home to buy a tail, and the purchase of her tail was contingent upon her selling her home. How many people do you know who have to literally sell their homes just to pay liability coverage? The federal government did nothing to address these concerns. The message to me is you, as a physician, don't count.

Q. Well, you are escaping. You are transitioning. I would definitely like to get out of private practice myself in the next year...

A. What you are doing is interesting. I have dabbled a little bit in medical writing and written several articles for journals. None of this paid anything, so I can't do it to pay the bills. I looked at every one of my options. I looked at becoming a sales rep. I looked at working for a drug company. I looked at trying to teach at the local community college where I was told I was too overqualified to teach. They felt intimidated by having an M.D. come in to teach anatomy to their nursing students. So I am overqualified for a lot of jobs and other jobs I am not qualified for at all. With this high level of education it can be really hard to transition out. Even getting an MBA is not the answer. If you ask several doctors who got MBA's, if it was worth it, you will get mixed answers.

I even looked into working for an online medical school, and found that the work load was too much. I couldn't do online medical school and take an ER call. I started to absolutely hated ER calls because they might bring in two or three patients every time, usually about 30% Medicaid patients. Maybe 10 or 15% would be commercial insurance, but by far most of it was Medicare. Every time I got a perforated diverticulitis in the emergency room, it was notoriously a Medicare patient who was really sick and would stay in the hospital for seven to ten days, so I would lose my weekend and never be able to leave town. It became a question of do I want to stay and take care of old people who believe that I exist to be at their beck-and-call, or do I just walk away from it all? I decided to walk away. It's just not healthy for me to stay in this profession.

DR. JAY CRUTCHFIELD

"Man cannot discover new oceans unless he has the courage to lose sight of the shore."

- Lord Chesterfield

"Dare to live another life!"
Dr. Zoe Deol, Freelance Guru

Dr. Zoe Deol is a surgeon. That is pretty much the only thing she is sure of these days. Somewhere between finishing her residency and completing her laparoscopic fellowship, September 11th occurred, and a close family friend died from the ravages of obesity. The emotional impact of these simultaneous events hurled Zoe in a new direction. Her private practice career evolved into a quest to surgically conquer obesity.

Much like other similar lager scale dreams (i.e. clean energy and world peace), her dreams were eventually crushed by the reality that those for whom she sacrificed her life to save were not as dedicated to saving themselves. Like a hamster on a wheel, she was never able to make any real progress no matter how hard or fast she ran. Zoe jumped off the wheel. Today, Dr. Deol is a freelance surgeon, a freelance writer, a freelance political aficionado, and a freelance photographer.

Q. Why did you become a physician?
A. My Dad is a surgeon. Out of his four children, I was the only one who followed him to his office, and even into the OR,

from a very young age. I felt more comfortable in a hospital than I did in school, or anywhere else.

Q. How did you choose your specialty practice?

A. Despite making my medical career choice obvious to everyone around me, I denied to everyone including myself that I was going to follow in my Dad's footsteps into the OR. However, I think it was always in my blood. In medical school, I gravitated towards the operating room. Even when I was doing a radiology rotation, I would coax a student who was covering surgery to give me their pager for the night. As a result I performed my first appendectomy as a third-year medical student. As a fourth-year medical student, I whip stitched closed a gaping gunshot hole in a 19-year-old boy's heart and did open cardiac massage. It was all over after that. I was hooked.

Q. Were you passionate about this decision?

A. VERY PASSIONATE. Operating is like a drug for me. The adrenaline rush leads to a surge of endorphins that puts me in a perpetual state of happiness until I leave the hospital. My surgical residency was, without a doubt, the best time of my life. I say this despite the fact that I trained in the days before "restricted work hours". My work weeks regularly exceeded 100 hours, but, when you are doing something you love, it isn't work. Every day, I laughed so hard that I cried.

For me, the hospital was like another planet, one that spun around in its own galaxy. When I went home, and came back down to earth, I would go through a decontamination shower, and then get debriefed by my husband. After that, I would go to sleep and dream about my next journey into the unknown. You have no idea what you will encounter, or how you will handle it. Even the oldest surgeon can be heard saying, "Wow, I've never seen that before!" But, like Jim Lovell on Apollo 13, when you rise to the occasion, and save a life as a result, there is no better feeling in the world.

Q. How did your career in this specialty go?

A. After completing my general surgery residency, I went on to do a fellowship in laparoscopic bariatric surgery. My intention was to hone my surgical skills to perfection. I am highly competitive, and laparoscopic bariatric surgery is known to be one of the most technically challenging procedures. I didn't intend to practice bariatric surgery when I finished. However, I did my fellowship in Chicago in 2001. I lived on the 32nd floor of a high rise, overlooking the Sears Tower and the Navy Pier. The simultaneous tragedy of September 11th, and the death of a close family friend from obesity related complications caused me to re-prioritize my life. I felt that I should use my bariatric training for its intended purpose, and battle obesity in memory of my dear friend. So I opened my own private practice in a suburb of Detroit, where I practiced solo for 7 years.

Q. Why did you decide to leave this practice?

A. I gave everything I had to my practice. I was on call every night, and never took a single vacation for seven years. I treated every one of my patients like my own child, and most of them acted like it. I noticed that my views on the disease of obesity changed over the years. I went from believing that it was a disease that was completely out of the control of the patient, to believing that it was more of a predisposition that one needed to be aware of. For example, with lung cancer, some people can smoke their whole life and never develop lung cancer. However, these people are in the minority. A far greater number of people are predisposed to developing lung cancer, so smoking is far more dangerous and will lead to cancer. Obesity is similar. There are few people who are not predisposed to obesity. There are those who can eat whatever they want, not exercise, and not gain weight. However, those people are in the minority. Most people are predisposed, so proper diet and exercise are mandatory to avoid obesity.

DR. ZOE DEOL

Unfortunately, I realized that none of my patients were interested in hearing that they had to make some lifestyle changes. They were coming to me for a "magic bullet" that would allow them to continue over eating all the wrong things, and continue avoiding exercise, while losing weight. It seemed like this had become the prevailing attitude for just about everyone in our society, "Have it all without any accountability." Sign the mortgage for that big expensive house even though you know you can't afford it. Rack up the credit card bills even though you know you can't pay them off. Invest in that impossible scheme even though you know it is too good to be true. The list goes on and on.

Q. What where the factors or events that drove you to change?

A. After seven years of sacrificing my life and almost my marriage for the sake of those who didn't want to lift a finger on their own behalf, I realized that I was sinking. Serendipitously, the auto industry crashed as a foreshadowing of what was to come in the general economy. Many people in Michigan lost their health benefits for obesity treatments long before the rest of the country fell victim. As a result, my practice went from making money, to breaking even, to paying out of pocket to keep my doors open. Like any true drug addict, I would beg, borrow, or steal to get my "fix" of surgery. My husband tried on two occasions to hold an intervention. It was his money after all that I was spending to care for those same patients who kept me away from him night and day.

It was my office manager who forced me to consider one of the many offers that had come my way to work for an independent bariatric surgery company in Chicago. She forced me to reflect on why I went into surgery, and why I was now unhappy. Apart from the specialty-specific details I have already mentioned, I realized that everything I had loved about my residency, now comprised only about 5% of my practice. The rest was all paperwork, documentation, avoiding lawsuits, and fighting with insurance companies.

No one prepares you for this reality in residency. You are given a skewed view of your future world. They hand you these rose-colored glasses through which you see your life revolving around the OR, probably for good reason. If they told you the truth about what your life would be like when you got out, I don't think many people would choose to go into surgery. CNBC recently featured a survey of America's most stressful jobs. Surgeon ranked number 4. I think that they have it wrong though, as far as their explanation of why it is stressful. The stress comes from all of the non-surgical details that drown you, rather than from the act of operating.

Q. Were you passionate about this decision?
A. I was NOT passionate about closing my practice. To me, it was like the death of a dream. Little did I know that my nightmare was about to get worse. I thought that accepting a position with a venture capital company would allow me to focus on the parts of my job that I loved, and leave all the administrative hassles to the company. Even though I was burning out on bariatrics. I hadn't considered doing anything else. However, I soon realized the danger of allowing non-medically trained people to make decisions that would direct the practices of a medical facility. Suffice to say that turned out to be a complete disaster, and I exited prior to any encounters with potential patients.

I returned to my home and my ever accepting and tolerant husband in Detroit. I realized that I was just given a chance at a "do-over." For the first time in years, I could go on vacation. I could drink a glass of wine with dinner. I could walk my dog in the middle of the day. I went to Dubai, Egypt, London, Paris, and Jordan. In Paris I got food poisoning and ended up in the hospital where an ER doctor from Colorado took care of me. She too had run away from home to avoid becoming another bitter American doctor.

I started writing down my thoughts on medicine and politics and eventually I was asked to publish these columns in a surgical magazine. While in Jordan, I interviewed hospital staff and created a feature piece comparing the U.S. health care crisis to the current medical system in Jordan. I had no idea I had this ability in me. I also started taking photographs that were later used in several different media outlets. I felt a huge weight lifted from my shoulders. I felt alive, young, and excited again. My husband and I became closer than we had ever been, and I no longer felt bitter and resentful that I gave all of myself to complete strangers, while hanging my loved ones out to dry. However, despite all the fun and excitement, the uncertainty of my future career brought with it a degree of anxiety that grew as the months ticked by.

Q. How did you discover your new career?

A. I started looking for non-clinical career options. I researched going back to school for an MBA. I joined websites for physicians looking for non-clinical careers. I interviewed for, and was offered a position as a content director for an Electronic Medical Records company. I even landed a consulting job with Glaxo-Smith-Kline for their weight loss product line. However, nothing that I "tried on" seemed to fit. There was no excitement for me in these steady paying positions. I knew what was happening. I was getting a craving for surgery again. My husband started getting nervous and began pacing around as he called my former office manager, Rebecca, who, to this day, is my best friend. She would "talk me down" each time I almost fell off the wagon.

In the end though, every addict has to confront his or her own demons. With the help of my husband and Rebecca, I started considering a clinical career, but on my own terms. I went on a quest for the Holy Grail, and would settle for nothing less. My first attempt was a second fellowship in Surgical Intensive Care. I figured that, after training, I could work with surgery patients, during regularly scheduled hours, and never have to deal with the hassles of an office or insurance companies. However, the closer I got to actually starting that fellowship, the worse things started to appear.

Doing a fellowship after age forty is not as easy as doing a fellowship straight out of residency. I would be leaving the happy home I had grown to love, for a paycheck that barely met minimum wage, to work hours similar to those I worked in residency. I was starting to sink again before I even started the fellowship. When it came right down to it, I couldn't do it. My fight or flight instinct took a hold of me and I fled. I ran back to the idea of freedom, but the anxiety and restlessness continued to grow. I was beginning to think I had PTSD (post traumatic stress disorder) from my years in private practice. Every time I thought of the implications of operating on a patient and the malpractice tail coverage for three years after your very last surgery, I had a panic attack. Somehow I had managed to escape that noose once because the venture capital company that hired me in Chicago paid for my tail coverage when I closed my private practice. This is such an obstacle to a physician considering leaving a practice. It may be the only reason they choose to stay.

Q. Did you have a business plan?

A. I never had any sort of plan. My main tool was networking. In private practice, I was always so wrapped up in my work that I never learned to network. That was something I now had to force myself to do. I used Google as a jumping off point and that eventually led me to the numerous groups of physicians who were looking for alternate career paths. Recently I connected with a local hospital, which had a unique position available: a surgical hospitalist. This relatively new hospital was looking for surgeons who were willing to work twelve hour, in-house shifts (6 pm to 6 am) covering all of the surgical patients. This freed up their regular surgical staff

DR. ZOE DEOL

from being dragged out of bed in the middle of the night. This is a non-operative position, so I am not sure how I will react, but I think I can handle it.

I realize I sound a bit like an alcoholic rationalizing how she can handle working as a bartender without taking a drink, but my employers weren't helping when they started pushing the one thing they knew I had a weakness for. The surgical director kept saying, "You know, if you want to join our regular surgical staff, we would love to have you, but no pressure!" Just as I was about to drink the Kool-Aid, he went too far by adding, "We are even starting a bariatric program." Like a bad memory, that was enough to snap me back into reality, and I said, "NO!" So, for now, I will start by working two nights a week, leaving the rest of the week open to pursue my new interests: writing, photography, and politics.

Q. During your clinical-to-non-clinical transition how was your income and cash flow affected?
A. During my world tour and soul searching phase, I did not have an income. Fortunately, I had savings from my job in Chicago.

Q. How does your income now compare to your previous practice income?
A. It is better. I get paid a flat fee for a 12-hour shift. No six month delay, filing claim after claim to the insurance company who always seemed to lose them. No overhead to pay. No malpractice to pay. The hospital covers that. So, on the surface it may appear that I am making less, but if I chose to work the same number of hours that I worked in private practice, I would be taking home much more.

Q. During your transition period, what were your toughest obstacles?
A. Closing my practice, in other words, being brave enough to

FREELANCE GURU

drop my security blanket even though it had become old, moldy, and smelly. That and admitting to myself that I wasn't happy doing what I was doing, and that I didn't want to do it anymore. It is tough to reconcile that a big portion of your life was spent slaving away at something that ultimately brought you no sense of gratification. The key is to turn that around and realize that every experience, even the bad ones, teach us something that will enable us to move on to the next great challenge.

Traveling and writing made me realize that the world is so big, and my time here is so short. If I had not dared to try something new, I would have spent my entire life in one little caged-up pen. In the end, that would have been far more disappointing to me than the notion that I had given up.

Q. How did your family and friends reacted to your transformation?

A. First and foremost is my husband. He stood by me through every "failure", through every doubt and insecurity, through every attempt at trying something new, and simply told me, "I love you no matter what you decide to do, even if you decide to sit on the couch and watch TV all day. I just want you to find something that makes you happy."

My father, on the other hand, accused me of becoming a housewife. He seemed ashamed and embarrassed by my choices and frequently fretted out loud about what his friends would think. Eventually, that forced us to discuss his expectations of his kids, and the importance of our happiness versus a career he could tell his friends about. In the end, we both realized that we had misinterpreted the other's feelings. My father was worried about my happiness. He never wanted me to be in the position of being financially dependent on my husband or anyone else. When he realized that I was truly happy, and that I wasn't sitting at home

DR. ZOE DEOL

eating bonbons, he grew more accepting of my new life. After all, he more than anyone truly understood the negative changes that medicine had gone through. He practiced surgery in its heyday, and witnessed firsthand its downward spiral. I remember when I told him I was going into surgery. I was surprised at his lack of enthusiasm. He already saw the writing on the wall.

My brother and my friends were all amazingly supportive. Never once did they make me feel like less of a person for walking away from a career and venturing into the unknown.

Q. Do you feel that your medical training has been helpful to you in your new career? Do you have any advice for other physicians contemplating change?

A. Stop thinking about change as failure, and start thinking of it as the brave and adventurous thing to do. On the business side: NETWORK. Go to every meeting, every function, every event, and mingle. Help others around you with their search, because that person may come back later and help you. Take a little time off to figure out what makes you happy, and then start researching ways to use your medical knowledge to work in that area. I could go on and on, but you get my drift!

Q. Any slogans to live by or core beliefs?

A. Dare to live another life!

8

"American medicine is still the best in the world when we focus on our ability to help others, and the worst in the world when we focus on making money. I think there is a problem when we focus too much on, 'What are you going to give me?' Instead of, 'What can I do for you?'"
Dr. Robin Dhillon, Trainer, Consultant, Living with MS

Dr. Robin Dhillon was born in Singapore and spent his first eleven years in Malaysia. His father, a physician, moved their family to "the land of opportunity" in 1970. After moving to the USA, Dr. Dhillon received a college education and a medical degree, with specialized training in cardiothoracic surgery.

Dr. Dhillon's surgical practice was interrupted when he developed Multiple Sclerosis (MS). He experienced a loss of sensation in his fingertips, along with several other symptoms like neuromuscular fatigue, short-term memory loss, and difficulties with balance. None of these affected his brain or long-term memory. As a result, Robin has been able to pursue several alternative jobs like teaching anatomy and physiology as well as the Spanish language. Dr. Dhillon consults on medical issues for attorneys, directs two plasma labs, and reviews medical issues for an association of automobile dealers.

Q. At the time that you developed MS, how did you go about seeking new employment? Were there opportunities on the web? Were there classes or courses for physicians who were having difficulty maintaining their practice for medical reasons?

A. Not really. I was out in the Pacific Northwest, so I moved back to Cleveland where my wife's family lived, giving her a support group. Because I had started my training here at Case Western University Hospital in Cleveland, I knew a few key people in academics at that time. After my recovery, which took me about eighteen months of depression and looking for other options, I ended up teaching anatomy at Case Western. I've done that ever since part-time. Then, just by keeping my ears open I found other opportunities. I work for a couple of lawyers. I also work at a blood blank or plasma center. And I'm always looking for more things to do. Basically I had no one to assist me.

Q. It sounds like you've had a difficult transition. How about being accepted? Did you have any problem being accepted as a physician with MS?

A. Not really, not within the community.

Q. Have you run into any other physicians who have had MS or similar diseases and weren't able to continue practicing?

A. No. Some people do practice without letting on that they have the illness and seem to do quite well depending on the illness.

Q. Any advice for others? How did you keep it together when you realized that you weren't going to be able to do surgery? How did you get through that time?

A. I still love medicine. I love working with people and helping them. Somehow that initial inspiration, which is what got me into medicine in the first place, is what has kept me going. I still find opportunities. It's not quite the same. Being a surgeon has its own rewards, both emotional and physical.

There is still a little bit of that when I find a way to help some-one. That's what has kept me going.

Q. Other physicians have just gotten tired of practicing medi-cine or fed up with economic or political problems. They feel stuck and decide to look for something else. Do you find you have more time to do other things?

A. I do and I don't. Once I start doing anything, it consumes me. I just don't have time to do all the things I want to do.

Q. Is there anything else you would like to comment on?

A. My approach has always been to keep the patient safe. I gave up surgery because I didn't feel that I could do that. And, if I couldn't do my best in surgery, I would be counter-productive. Yet, there are still places where I can contribute on a knowledge basis. Most lay people don't have our un-derstanding of illnesses and so on. They don't have quite the same understanding of appendicitis that you or I have. It helps to have an interpreter. That's how I see my role now, as an interpreter.

Q. So it helps for you to be the interpreter?

A. This struck me over and over again, as I got off-the-beaten path of surgery. American medicine is still the best in the world when we focus on our ability to help others, and the worst in the world when we focus on making money. I think there is a problem when we focus too much on, "What are you going to give me?" Instead of, "What can I do for you?"

DR. ROBIN DHILLON

"What you are will show in what you do."
                                    - Thomas Edison

"Simply because they are doctors, they think they bring some inherent value when in fact it's really about delivery. It's about what you can manage, what you can deliver, and how you can turn that into business. Those are really important aspects. Business is about being in business, not about collecting people with a lot of degrees."

Dr. Harry Greenspun, Chief Medical Officer

DR. HARRY GREENSPUN

Harry Greenspun, MD, is the Chief Medical Officer of Dell Services, providing strategic leadership with a clinical perspective. He has held a diverse range of clinical and executive roles across the healthcare industry, giving him a unique perspective on the challenges and opportunities faced in health IT.

Over the course of his career, Dr. Greenspun has held many key roles in implementing company-and industry-wide policy. Prior to working for Dell Services, he served as Chief Medical Officer for Northrop Grumman Corporation, where he provided subject matter expertise, thought leadership, and strategic direction for the company. More than a decade ago, Dr. Greenspun founded a company that tracked clinical outcomes in cardiac surgery, which later became the healthcare practice of an open source software company.

Dr. Greenspun has been both an educator and consultant throughout his career, sharing his expertise for several organizations, including the Advisory Board Company and serving on advisory boards for Tufts University, George Mason University, Deloitte, and BNA. As a chairman of the Health Information Management Systems Society's (HIMSS) Government Relations Roundtable and co-chair of the HIMSS task force responsible for creating the white paper entitled, "Enabling Healthcare Reform Using Information Technology," Dr. Greenspun has made recommendations to the Obama administration and Congress on the importance of health IT investment to the nation. Dr. Greenspun is actively involved in promoting the use of health information technology on a global scale and serves on the World Economic Forum's Global Health Advisory Board. He has been quoted extensively in the media and among analysts on this topic and is seen as a thought leader among industry leaders. He is co-author of the book entitled, "Reengineering Healthcare" with Jim Champy.

Dr. Greenspun received his bachelor's degree from Harvard University, his medical degree from the University of Maryland, and completed his residency and fellowship at Johns Hopkins Hospital, where he served as chief resident in the Department of Anesthesiology and Critical Care Medicine. As a cardiac anesthesiologist, he practiced in major academic medical centers, as well as community hospitals. Dr. Greenspun has also been named one of the Top 10 Healthcare IT Game Changers to Watch by ExecutiveBiz.com and one of the 50 Most Powerful Physician Executives by Modern Healthcare.

CHIEF MEDICAL OFFICER

Q. I want to start off with why you were attracted to medicine in the first place, and then why you were attracted away from it eventually?

A. Even as kid, from about 5th grade on, I wanted to be a doctor. I was interested in emergency medicine and trauma. I was even a firefighter in high school, so I went to college knowing that I wanted to be a doctor. While I was in college, I did my pre-med requirements, but I spent most of my time doing psychology, architecture, and ancient Greek history. Those were the areas I focused on at Harvard.

Then, because I wanted to be a trauma surgeon, my first choice was University of Maryland. They have a shock trauma unit there. I went to Maryland and had a nice career there. I was class president, but I quickly realized that trauma was not what I had hoped it would be, though I did like surgery. I liked the immediacy of the operating room so I got interested in anesthesia. I went off to Hopkins to do my residency and wound up specializing in cardiac. I liked the collaborative aspect of it. I also liked the technology and the intensity of it. We were doing minimally invasive heart surgery when it was new, beating heart cardiac surgery.

We were also collecting data on each patient. I think there were only about forty centers worldwide doing that. We had these paper forms to fill out, and at the time my brother was at MIT doing database work. I realized there was a better way of doing this. So I got some of his graduate students to build an internet-based registry. This was in the early '90s, back when the internet was becoming more interesting. I quickly realized this would be a great idea for a business. I left Hopkins then. I had a private practice in community hospitals in Baltimore as a full-time cardiac anesthesiologist, while also trying to get a business off the ground. I did manage to get that business to grow.

Well, it was less of an achievement than total lack of sleep. I

Dr. Harry Greenspun

found I could get by with less and less sleep. I had a baby at home. I had a lot going on and I decided that if I didn't sleep, then I could make it all happen. I got interested in business and managed to get some good, professional management experience in my company. It was a very small internet start-up, like so many were. I was fortunate to get a guy who was a Harvard business school graduate to be my CEO. I got my business education by being an entrepreneur. I was fascinated and really enjoyed it. So I continued to practice medicine at a constantly decreasing rate.

One of the beauties of anesthesiology and the ER is you can really do it part-time and still maintain your practice. I managed to negotiate a 50% clinical position at a hospital in Washington D.C. as my business grew. Then ultimately by 1999 I realized that if I was going to have to make my business work. So I quit my full-time single practice, but continued to moonlight for a couple reasons. I didn't really want to quit my day job, because what I was doing was so risky. At the time, one of the first questions physicians would ask me about my business was, "Are you a practicing physician?" It was very important early in my career that I appear to be a real doctor in their eyes.

So my company grew, and became the health care vertical of a larger company and eventually got acquired. After the acquisition, I realized the mission of the acquiring company was not the direction I wanted to go in. It wasn't really health care and not what I saw myself doing.

But because I had maintained my practice, and they were desperate for more help, I was quickly able to get back into full-time clinical practice. I worked my way up in various hospitals, while using what I had learned in the business world to improve how we ran our hospital. After about a year of that, I began to get bored with the traditional environment. While it has the life and death mission aspect, there's no dynamic growth there. Some places are entrepreneurial and business oriented, but I missed that side of it.

I had been fielding calls from different recruiters, and got called by an advisory board which was very big in health care. They were looking for physicians to teach other physicians about business management. It seemed right up my alley, so I took that position but still maintained a very small amount of my clinical work. I wound up traveling all around the country to hospitals, large and small, teaching physician groups about communication, finance and chain management. The docs were so welcoming of a business education. They desperately needed it and wished they had had it earlier.

This gave me a national perspective on health care that I hadn't had before, but I was on the road six out of seven days of the week. I decided I wanted a more stable environment for my family, so I reached out to some executive recruiters that I knew and wound up getting recruited in to help build the health care practice of one of the larger executive recruiters. I did that for a while and that helped me understand a couple things: how to put together a successful team, how to evaluate individuals for their ability to manage other people, how to look at the business needs of an organization from both a clinical and business perspective, how to sell professional services, how to network appropriately, and how to make all that work together. I enjoyed that a lot, but again, as a physician, unless you are really close to health care, it can feel like you are not doing what you thought you should be doing.

At that stage I got recruited to be the chief medical officer. North Bremond is obviously an enormous defense contractor, and they did a large business in health care for the VA. They are the number one contractor with the CDC, doing a lot of public health work, and they also work with Pharma.

Dr. Harry Greenspun

What they needed was somebody who understood all those different realms and could be the appropriate thought leader for the group. It was a really nice fit, because I had lots of experience, I had been a professional speaker and facilitator and I brought a lot of credibility to a group that was largely made up of IT staff, not medical people. That was very interesting.

Q. Did your education in business include any formal training at this point, or just real world training?

A. Aside from some of the stuff I was teaching at the advisory board, I had no formal business training except running companies and being involved that way. When you have worked with a publicly traded company and you are analyzing deals that your group may want to acquire, you learn a lot about business pretty quickly. You also learn that finance rules. In big business, the more you understand finance, the higher up you can go in the organization. I spent a lot of time learning about finance with our CFO, and getting him to teach me about what the numbers really mean.

Q. What advice do you have for other docs in transition? Would you recommend that they get formal business training or do it like you did?

A. I was very lucky and have found great success in industry, but for most doctors, a deeper understanding of finance is essential. Have they actually ever managed other people? Have they been responsible for a P and L of any size? Most doctors over-estimate their value to an organization. Simply because they are doctors, they think they bring some inherent value when in fact it's really about delivery. It's about what you can manage, what you can deliver, and how you can turn that into business. Those are really important aspects. Business is about being in business, not about collecting people with a lot of degrees. It's about what you are trying to do and what you are managing. If all you can do is stand around being a doctor, in the business world there are limited places for you.

Q. So a doctor needs to be on the team, and he may not be the captain?

A. Yes. You need to understand how it works. You need to understand how the doctor adds value to every other person on the team. I think that is a mistake that I made early in my career, trying to figure out what I should do as opposed to going to my unit business leader and asking them, "How can I help you? What do you need from me?" I got great advice from some of those people. Some of them wanted me to build relationships. Others wanted me to write more articles, while others wanted me to get out in front of large groups. Some of them wanted me to meet with their teams and explain to them what it all means and why we were doing it. All of them wanted different things and not necessarily what I would have predicted. That was probably my best move. So now, when I move on to other roles, the first thing I do is I meet with all of the major business unit leaders and senior executives and say, "How can I help you? What do you want from someone in this role?"

Q. You have to listen to other people on your team?

A. Yes. So, I was up north for a couple years and then I got recruited to Perot Systems, which was one of the largest providers of IG services in the private section, and actually got me closer to real care, working with hospitals. We do a lot of work internationally, so I have spent time in the UK and China. We are deploying electronic health records across the entire country of Jordan.

One of the things I learned at Russell Reynolds is you've got to network appropriately. You've got to get involved in activities where people start to recognize you as a real expert and thought leader, so I became the chairman of the a government relations round table. I got involved in health care policy, was asked to co-chair a couple task forces, and I began to get known. I began to sell my personal brand. I began to write more, get recognized more, and use my position of thought leadership in the social media. Now people come to me or at least recognize me as a guy who knows a lot of different things.

Even if I had never written or spoken about something, they might think that I'm a guy who might know something or knows someone who does. I was really quite effective because in this last round of health care reform, I was voted #18 of the 50 most powerful executives. The irony is that I had very little power, but I do have a lot of influence. I have a lot of connections that has been the result of systematically making sure that I am connected at the right levels with the right people, but more importantly, I bring value to them with new information.

A mistake a lot of doctors make is they expect people to find them. They are not good at networking or at differentiating themselves from anybody else who is interested in leading traditional clinical practice or going into something else.

Q. What about the future? Do you see more of an emphasis on business education in medical school, so that the students get exposed earlier and may even take rotations with business leaders?

A. Having taught business to doctors for years, uniformly the message from them was, "I wish I had had this kind of education in medical school." I am a strong believer in physician education and leadership development. One of the big things going on right now is that there is inherent value in teaching physician leadership. There are not enough physicians with sufficient leadership and business skills to be really effective.

It's a great time to be a physician leader or a physician who

CHIEF MEDICAL OFFICER

wants to get into leadership positions. What I tell a lot of doctors is to get leadership training and get into leadership positions, even in their hospital or own group, so that they can demonstrate that they have some skills that are transferable. So they have a track record.

I think what hospitals and practices want, is not more business people. We've got lots and lots of business people. What we need are physician leaders who understand business, and some of these very successful businesspeople. That's in clinical medicine from Lasik to radiology centers. There are lots of people who have made a lot of money as physician businessmen, but there's so much work going on in health care right now where they need physicians who are effective leaders.

Q. Do you have any projects going on in the future or any topics that you have a burning desire to comment on?

A. I am in the center of the firestorm of health care reform. When I think of all the changes that are coming in the next few years, between the implementation of health care reform to all the changes in accountable care organizations and reimbursement changes, plus huge cuts in Medicare and Medicaid, there is a desperate need for strong leadership by physicians, both within clinical care and within all the associated agencies and companies that serve it. It's a terrific opportunity. I think there's a lot there.

I do have one caution. I get asked by a lot of really young docs if they should go into business. What I tell them is that until you have actually been in practice, it will be hard for you to find credibility as a physician in business. You will be a business person with an MD, but health care is a very credential-focused organization. For better or for worse, you want to know whether the physician, physician leader, or CEO of a hospital you are speaking to understands the pressures of dealing with primary care, caring for patients and

Dr. Harry Greenspun

keeping a practice in business. Those are the things they want to know. If you go straight from your internship off to business school, just be aware when people start asking about your background and experience, they can quickly tell whether you have clinical experience.

Some ask me if they should go to medical school to have a good business career and I think, "That's insane!" When you think about the suffering you go through, you have got to really want to become a doctor to go through medical school. Don't do it as a way of getting a better business job. It's just too hard. You may ruin the rest of your life in the process just for credentials. You are better off just going into business and then getting an M.A. in health administration, rather than slaving through an MD if your heart is not in it.

I think most don't appreciate how very rewarding a career can be as a physician executive, and I am probably your best example. I went from being an anesthesiologist, with a one on one relationship with each patient. I now impact the health of hundreds of millions of people around the world.

For me, this is no less rewarding than getting someone through an emergency surgery. It's definitely different, but it's not like it's the dark side. It's not like I have given up on health care or medicine or that I've sold my soul. It can be extremely rewarding, progressive, and challenging. On a day-by-day basis it's extremely interesting.

"I think docs need to realize that if they were smart enough to get into medical school, they are probably smarter than 90 to 95% of the general population. So they do have the ability to do many things other than medicine. Don't sell yourself short."
Dr. Alan Jacobson, Navy Veteran - Operation Desert Storm

Dr. Jacobson grew up in Augusta, Georgia. He obtained a BA at Bowdoin College in Brunswick, ME and his M.D. at the Medical College of Georgia. He completed a psychiatry residency at the University of Connecticut and a neurology residency at Albany Medical Center. He is board certified in both specialties. Dr. Jacobson served on active duty with the Navy between 1975-1977 at the Naval Submarine Medical Center in Groton, CT., and was recalled for Operation Desert Storm. He was in private practice in Texas during the 1980's and in Maine in the 1990's.

Q. When did you start your medical career?
A. I graduated from medical school in 1972 and then did a three
   year residency in psychiatry, finishing in 1975. Next I had a
   two year commitment with the United States Navy, and I did
   a second residency in neurology from 1977 to 1980. I main-

DR. ALAN JACOBSON

81

tained a private practice from 1980 until 2000.

Q. Why did you decide to go to medical school and become a physician in the first place? What attracted you to the profession?

A. My father and his brothers were all health professionals. He and one of his brothers were dentists, and his older brother was a physician, so there was a familial influence. My Dad encouraged me to go to medical school. One of the reasons my Dad thought I should be a physician is, "You are your own boss." You have control over your life. Then another factor was how many of my college friends chose to go into pre-med. I saw that as a challenge, just to see if I could actually get into medical school.

Q. So what helped to change your mind? When did you decide you needed to get out of clinical medicine and go into something else?

A. During the 1990s it became more apparent. My stress level was increasing as my professional gratification was decreasing, and my income had leveled off. I had been in practice in Texas during the 1980s, and when I left for the Gulf War I had to close my practice. Then, when I came back, I had to start all over from scratch. I also saw the dangers that were coming in health care reform and decided that I didn't want to continue.

My practice was intruding greatly into my personal life. I had no quality of life because the doctor I was cross-covering with was very unreliable so the burden of most of the work fell on me. I was getting calls even when I wasn't on call, so it had turned into a 24/7 kind of job. It got to the point where I couldn't go anywhere or do anything without my beeper going off. I was feeling pretty stressed.

Q. What steps did you take to find your way out?

A. I started looking around to see what might be out there, and

I saw a classified ad in the New England Journal of Medicine from Udim Providence Insurance Company. They were looking to hire several doctors. They listed all the specialties they were looking for. Ironically they had almost every specialty except neurology, and maybe pediatrics. But I sent them a letter and explained to them why I thought it would be helpful if they had a neurologist working for them. I didn't hear anything back. Then I met a doctor one day at the Naval Reserve Center and started talking to him. He was working at Udim part-time. So we started talking and he said, "No problem," and three days later I got a call from one of the medical directors. They called me in for an interview and then offered me a job.

So I closed my practice. They wanted me full-time, but I was thinking of only working for them half-time and maintaining my practice. Then I talked to a friend of mine and said, "What if I don't like it?" And he said, "Well, do you like what you are doing now?" And I said, "No." So he said, "Well, then you have nothing to lose." When I thought about it later, I thought, "Right – what's the worst thing that can happen? I will just have to go back and start my practice all over again, and I have already done that a couple of times. So I closed my office within a couple of months and I went to work for Udim.

The pay was competitive with what I was making in practice, plus there were nice fringe benefits like more time off and no on-call or weekends. They also provided me with a budget for continuing education and pension plans. From an overall standpoint it was a step up. So I worked as an employee for about five years, but over time I started getting offers for contract work from other companies. So after five years I left Udim, and have just been working on a contract basis with several insurance companies ever since. I just bill by the hour and the nice thing about it is, I can work as many hours as I want or as few as I want and reimbursement is 100%.

So if I complete the work within two weeks, I have a direct deposit into my account. It's been a lot less stressful, and I have virtually no overhead. Before, in practice, my overhead got up to 40% of my growth, and here it's about 3%. I have an insurance policy, what they call errors and omissions, and I maintain my medical license by doing continuing education, but I don't have any employees and I don't have an office. I think my out-of-pocket expenses, even with my car lease, are probably around $12,000 to $14,000 a year.

Q. It sounds like you eventually became your own boss, just like your father suggested.

A. My father, yeah. One of the things I learned over time is you are really not your own boss when you are in private practice. In fact, it is quite the opposite. I found out I had more bosses in private practice, than I did when I was in the Navy. When I was in the Navy I had one boss, the OIC of the department. That was it. As long as I kept him happy everything was fine, but in practice you are responsible for federal government and agencies, you have the state and their requirements, and you have to keep the referring doctors happy. Obviously, the patients are your boss, and the private insurance companies are your boss. It's to the point where they dictate what you are going to get reimbursed for your work. So I actually had a lot of bosses and I wasn't my own boss at all.

Q. Are you an independent medical examiner? How would you describe your role, your career?

A. Well, it's kind of like an investigator. I look at disability claims and at medical records and reports and my role is really to see if there is or is not medical support for somebody filing a disability claim. I have to analyze medical records, but then there is also collateral information I have to look at, including looking at surveillance videos to see if their behavior when they are out and about is substantially different from their behavior in a doctor's office. I also compare medical records between providers because sometimes a patient will go into one doctor's office with one symptom and then go to another doctor's office with a totally different set of problems. I look to see if everything is credible and consistent.

Q. So it sounds like you are in charge of your workload. You can schedule when you want to work to a certain extent?

A. Yes, no one is calling me in the middle of the night, but I do have plenty of work. I have more work than I can handle. I go in and there's a big pile I need to plow through. There are no time constraints. I can spend as much time as I need to review a claim, which on average takes about four hours, but it can be as little as one hour. I had one where I had to spend two days reviewing all the lengthy, detailed medical documentation. It's almost like detective work. I just take what I learned in medical school and apply it in a non-medical arena.

Q. Do you have any advice or cautions for someone who might want to transition out of clinical into this type of investigative medicine?

A. I think docs need to realize that if they were smart enough to get into medical school, they are probably smarter than 90 to 95% of the general population. So they do have the ability to do many things other than medicine. Don't sell yourself short. I think sometimes doctors get so entrenched, that they develop this fear of leaving or changing careers. They may become paralyzed, because they are just so financially embedded in what they are doing that it can feel difficult to bail out. But you have to have confidence in yourself and faith that you can do this. The only person holding you back is you, with the possible exception of your spouse. My spouse is very supportive. She encouraged me to take the leap. She has always been very supportive of anything I wanted to do.

I hate to get off onto an economic tangent, but it really is pure capitalism. Capitalism is all about risk. If you are not willing to take a risk, then you are not going to reap the rewards. But if you are willing to take that risk, you will see rewards. When you consider the high level of education and training of most physicians, the actual risk is probably lower than most who decide to change careers.

Q. What kinds of obstacles did you face as you transitioned to your work in insurance?

A. There was a culture shock for me in the first few months. The company I went to work for was about 20 miles away from where I lived, but it wasn't a bad drive. At least I knew I would go in every morning and return home at night. I didn't have to worry about going back in again late at night or having to work on weekends. But for the first six months I did have some difficulty adapting to the drop in my stress level. I kept pinching myself and saying, "Can this be for real? You mean I can have a different life?" I mean, if you figure I started medical school in 1968 and there's just been this constant stress level at least from your 3rd year and definitely through residency, I just got conditioned to a very high level of stress. When that goes away I felt a little bit of difficulty adjusting to the idea that I could actually have a personal life and there is such a thing as high quality of life that I hadn't experienced in years, if ever.

Q. Any slogans or principles that have gotten you through the tough times? Anything else you might like to share?

A. I can't think of any slogans. I think the basics are you have to believe in yourself and pursue your own dreams. Go after your dreams and don't let yourself get bogged down in self-pity if you are unhappy. I am sure there are physicians out there who are one hundred percent satisfied with their work, and for them I would strongly suggest they stay where they are. But for those who don't feel that kind of gratification anymore, or those who find it a burden or a chore, I think you need to have faith in yourself that you do have the ability to do something else. My suspicion is things are probably going to be getting worse with healthcare reform.

It's not just a question of "leaving clinical medicine." You need to be striving for something and not just running away from something. So the idea is what is it you are striving for? What do you want to achieve? For me it was a certain quality of life. Now I just have so much more free time. I feel so much better emotionally and mentally than I did before. It's hard to describe.

Dr. Alan Jacobson

"Learning is about more than simply acquiring new knowledge and insights; it is also crucial to unlearn old knowledge that has outlived its relevance. Thus, forgetting is probably at least as important as learning."

- Gary Ryan Blair

"The creative process is about expanding options, coming up with a whole new way of looking at things, thinking of many different options, taking one possibility and expanding it out. That is what I love about business development."

Dr. Philippa Kennealy, The Entrepreneurial MD

Philippa Kennealy MD MPH CPCC PCC is founder and president of The Entrepreneurial MD, the "home" for physicians who want to become thriving entrepreneurs.

As an ICF-certified business coach, and physician educator, she is passionate about helping medical doctors reconnect to their sense of purpose and direction through applying creative thought, strategy and discipline to the development of their medical practices or non-clinical businesses.

Q. Please tell me a little bit about your upbringing.

A. I was raised in South Africa, the eldest of three children, by two professionals, one a teacher and the other an engineer. We had a very lovely home, and my father was gender-blind in most ways. He believed I should be able to do anything I wanted to with my life. I was fortunate. I began my adventure by going to live with a family in Costa Rica as an exchange student at age sixteen. I didn't see or speak to my family for an entire year. We only communicated by mail.

Q. How did you find your way to medicine?

A. I was very poorly prepared in terms of career opportunities. I really did not know what I wanted to do. I didn't give it much thought while I was away in Costa Rica. My Dad decided that I would come back and go to the university. He put in some applications for me, just in case I wanted to go to the local university. When I arrived back in South Africa, he asked me what I wanted to do. I told him I would go to the local university. So he said, "In that case, I only put in two applications for you, one in physical therapy and one in medicine." I thought, physical therapy doesn't sound like me, so maybe I'll do medicine. That's how I ended up in medicine.

Q. How did you choose your specialty?

A. Again, there is nothing straightforward about any of my choices. I chose my specialty by default. I originally trained in South Africa and had actually chosen pathology as my specialty, but discovered within a year that I didn't like pathology. I gave myself time off to go to work in the bush in Zimbabwe for what was going to be one year, but ended up working three years as a general practitioner.

On my return to South Africa, I was trying to decide what to do next with my life and got the opportunity to visit the United States while I was killing time. I came to the United States and fell in love and moved to the United States. At that time, I thought that I loved dermatology, but when I looked into it and saw how much training was involved, I decided to choose family medicine. Again, I was backed into this career option rather than directly selecting it myself.

THE ENTREPRENEURIAL MD

Q. Did you enjoy being a family physician in the United States?

A. It was really good for a time. I did my training in Santa Monica and then joined a very good practice in there, building a very solid practice. I enjoyed the work enormously in the beginning, and then woke up one day and the very nature of medicine was changing before my eyes. It was moving in the direction of an HMO environment. The amount of oversight and permission needed to order any particular procedure had increased dramatically. The constant adjudication of how I practice medicine was really irksome to me. On top of that, the patients were becoming restless and frustrated and taking a lot of their frustrations out on me. One day I realized I was just not having fun anymore.

I looked around to see what my alternative options were, and came across a masters degree in Public Health. It was a new program being started at UCLA, an executive-type degree. It was really fascinating degree in health care administration and policy. My husband and I went and took the course together. Midway through that two year course I had the opportunity to apply for a medical director position at Santa Monica Hospital. It became the Santa Monica/UCLA Medical Center. I hadn't really anticipated going in that direction.

Q. Quite a big jump, wasn't it?

A. It was. It was an extension of a lot of work I'd been doing in practice. I had been quite active on various committees in local hospitals and on the board of directors at one hospital. I found myself attracted to this non-clinical administrative role, a more influential role as a physician executive. That role then evolved into the CEO of the hospital.

That launched my non-clinical executive career in a very short time. I started out doing medical practice part-time, and administrative the rest. Within a very short time it became obvious that this was completely impractical, because

Dr. Philippa Kennealy

I couldn't get the work done, and I thought they were really underutilizing my administrative abilities. I was able to get my boss to see that I could make a much bigger contribution administratively. But I felt constrained because I had to run back to the office for half of the week. When I got back to my medical practice, every phone call that had come in that week would be delayed and I'd walk into these huge piles of charts on my desk. My partners were busy and couldn't handle anything non-urgent. My life became completely non-clinical and I made a decision within one month that this was a sign. It was time to get out of clinical practice altogether. So I left back in 1996.

Q. And your lifestyle with this new career?

A. It was very acceptable. Quite honestly it wasn't vastly different from being in practice, although I did love giving up being on-call. We had administrative calls, but it was completely different. Within a few months of being in my new role, I was on the administrative call team, but there really wasn't much to that. What a dramatic change in lifestyle. As for the hours during the day, I worked fairly long hours and there were lots of meetings and running back and forth between the community hospital and UCLA, but my daytime hours didn't change that much.

Q. What passion did this fulfill for you, being an executive rather than a practitioner?

A. That's a good question, because for me it did fulfill the passion of learning something new everyday. Part of my decision-making process for leaving the clinical side was spent in asking, "What will I miss about clinical practice?" When I boiled it down, it came down to interpersonal relationships. It wasn't important for me to lay a stethoscope on someone. It wasn't important for me to remove a piece of skin for a skin biopsy or do a pap smear. While that was enjoyable, it wasn't what attracted me to the clinical side of things. What I really loved was the capacity to interact with patients. To

THE ENTREPRENEURIAL MD

me that seems like a plausible experience.

As long as I went to a job that committed me to having those types of engagements with other people, that was what I really needed. This job opportunity was a new way of interacting with my colleagues, my physicians' colleagues and with the administrative team. So while the work itself was interesting, it wasn't the real passion. The passion was being interactive with people in the same sorts of ways. It was less intimate than practicing family medicine. That's ultimately why I was attracted to coaching, my current business, because I gave me the privilege of maintaining those intimate relationships again. I really love relationships where I can experience close intimacy, be genuinely helpful to someone, and get something out of my work. Then, I don't have any of the nonsense that goes along with dealing with the insurance stuff.

Q. Is that your current role, working as a coach? Is that how you would describe your role?

A. My career has evolved several steps beyond hospital administration. From that, I went into an internet start-up at the start of the dot com boom. I was intrigued by what was going on, and when a company called me, I just couldn't resist. I had to go. I became an executive vice-president for an internet start-up company, where I worked in the clinical oversight role. We were working with clinical online products we were creating. The clinical oversight as it translates through the screenwriting, the coding and programming processes. We would make sure that it was still accurate by the time it emerged as an online program. I loved that work. That was a passion for me.

In that job I discovered this thing called coaching, because I had an online coaching program to get through. I had never heard of coaching. So, I did all the research I needed to and slowly learned this was the career for me. I love being paid to talk to someone and listen, and not have to worry about the other stuff. It was fabulous. I figured it would be my retirement career. Little did I know my company was about to go under. I did another project for a different company for a year, and then decided it was time to commit. I put my money where my mouth was, and become a coach.

Q. So this seems to be really lighting your fire now. This is driving you?

A. Very much so. I love this work. It's deeply meaningful to me. It had a wonderful ripple effect, because instead of just helping people one at a time, I help one person who then helps all sorts of other people. I feel I have a much better ripple effect then I ever felt I had as a clinician.

Q. If others were interested in going in this direction, would they need any extra training for your new kind of work?

A. Yes. Coaching is still very open right now. You can become a coach by just sticking up a shingle and saying you're a coach. It's perfectly acceptable. My sense is that it's trending in the direction of increased professionalism, just like the early days of medicine year ago, and psychology. My sense is that coaching is going to come under increasing pressure to regulate itself and require credentialing. I received excellent training. It was very interesting for me, because as a family physician I was somewhat arrogant going into coaching. I was deeply humbled by my own coaching training. I learned a different way to interact with people and be of assistance. I learned a great deal. I completed the training and then a coaching certification process.

Q. Where was that?

A. Through the Coaches Training Institute, one of the early coaching schools. It has been around since the early days of formalized coaching training. It was one of the first two or three schools ever started, and had a very well-run program.

Q. Where was that located?

A. It is located out of northern California, but many different cities host training sessions. I moved down to Los Angeles within a few months of making inquiries. I trained here in Los Angeles, but they have numerous training programs all over the United States and now they have it in other countries as well.

Q. How about the transition period? How was your income and cash flow affected?

A. Tremendously. In my first year as a coach I made negative $11,000. There is definitely some financial planning involved in making this type of transition. It took me about four years to make the same kind of income I was making as a family physician.

To be quite honest, if I had to do it all over again, knowing what I know now, I could get my income up much faster. There was a very long, steep learning curve for me. There was no one out there teaching me how to build the kind of business that I wanted. Now there are a lot of coaches teaching coaches how to make money.

The thing about coaching is that most coaches make on average $30,000-$45,000 per year, which was obviously not an acceptable trade-off for me being in family practice and then as a hospital administrator. It took me quite some time to learn what it is to really run the business, how to market effectively and communicate the value proposition of coaching. Now that I've been able to figure this out, I can condense my experience and knowledge into instructing physicians who wish to become coaches. It will be a much quicker, steeper learning curve where they can get the benefits of all the mistakes I made and not have to make them themselves.

Q. Besides the cash flow, did you have any other obstacles?

A. The biggest obstacle was just learning about business and

DR. PHILIPPA KENNEALY

marketing. I came into that feeling overwhelmed with the thought of having to go out and sell myself. I can't really think of something as nebulous as coaching. Coaching is an experience rather than something you can easily describe. I had to figure out how to translate this into outcomes for people. I had to learn what marketing was all about. For me, the biggest obstacle has been the learning curve of how to attract clients.

Q. Where do you get that information and education?
A. I literally became as student. You cannot believe what is on my bookshelf. I took many magazines, read blogs, took some online training, and group coaching programs. All the way through I had my own business coach as well, really different business coaching according to different needs I had at the time. I had a coach to help me with branding for a while, and then a coach to help me get the operational part of my website up and running. All the way along I was learning, learning, learning.

Q. That is a good reminder. As physicians we are used to that.
A. Which is why this is a great career for a physician! First of all this is a natural niche for a lot of physician skills, and a lot of the drive that makes someone want to become a physician in the first place. Secondly, there is a phenomenal opportunity to keep learning.

I found it very interesting to wake up one day and discover that as much as I was enjoying the coaching, I also loved the business development piece. It was about that same time that I made the decision to shift from general physician coaching to a tighter niche, where I help physicians start their own businesses and teach them how to become more entrepreneurial. I teach this from the perspective, not so much of how to create a livelihood, but more, how to use this as a vehicle to express our creativity.

THE ENTREPRENEURIAL MD

The one contrast I noticed when I worked in a clinical practice, was the reductive way of thinking. You need to take a broad array of possibilities and come out with one diagnosis. You are constantly narrowing down your process. In a way it is the opposite of the creative process. The creative process is about expanding options, coming up with a whole new way of looking at things, thinking of many different options, taking one possibility and expanding it out. That is what I love about business development. If you are your own boss, you get to create and design and test and evaluate. That is a big part of being human, and it's missing for so many doctors, which is why so many are frustrated on the job.

Q. That is a very good point! We do lose the opportunity to be creative in medicine, but we can use our creativity in some other way, as you have done. What were some of your biggest breakthroughs while establishing a coaching business? What do you feel you've contributed?

A. I would say my bragging rights have been two-fold. The first is to feel that I deliver a really good service. In a way, that's an extension of what I did as a family physician. I feel like I am a good coach. I have very satisfied clients who are making great strides and changing their lives and so that feels good.

Then the second bragging right is to have acquired this whole other layer of knowledge and have reached a stage where I'm helping my clients. I'm sometimes blown away with what is inside my brain. Where does it all come from, and how have all of my various experiences added up to this type of wisdom in my life? It sometimes shocks me. How did I know that? Where did I learn that? Where did this come from? What I love about this professional choice is that it gives me huge avenues for unpacking some of my wisdom, and sharing it. I love handing it on.

Q. I understand what you are saying. What about those doctors who are contemplating change?

A. There is a dual process that needs to go on. Number one is an internal process that needs to happen. It's not going to come from the outside. They need to be a deeply reflective, self-evaluative person. They may reach a point where they feel like they've made a mistake with their career. They're not happy or they're miserable, and they realize it has been a very costly journey for them to reach that place. They don't want to make another mistake. The only way of avoiding that in your middle years, is to do some deep internal work and be able to answer questions.

When I went into medicine I did not have a moment of self-reflection about whether it was for me. But at the point at which I was making a new career choice, I was deeply reflective about what I wanted next, what was missing, what was important to me, what did I value, and what was the vision I wanted to create? That is where I always begin with new clients. I take them on an inner-reflective journey of uncovering and articulating values, where they identify their purpose, almost like a personal mission statement. They need to have a vision of: "Who am I becoming in this process? How am I going to respect myself in becoming this person? And how is this going to all unfold?" So, there is this internal process.

Then, there is this external process of finding out what is out there. Networking is key, because you begin to have conversations with those who do not work in medicine. This exposes you to many new opportunities. We look at any training that might be needed to close the skills gaps.

I use the three-legged stool model. Or, a better way to think of it is three intersecting circles in a Venn diagram. The first circle is your passion and interest: what do you really love?

THE ENTREPRENEURIAL MD

What deeply moves you? If you had unlimited money, how would you chose to spend your days and why? So, passion and interest is one circle. The next circle is skill, power and ability. What have you been trained to do? What are you innately good at? What has experience taught you?

The third circle is the marketability piece. How could I get paid to do what it is I love? You need to find that point where all three of those overlap. Sometimes you might close the skills gap. Hopefully you will be able to engage your greatest passion, but sometimes you may not be able to make it marketable in the short term. Sometimes you have to have a short term and a long-term plan.

Ultimately you may want to be there and end up there, but in the beginning you may have to start out here. So, it is very much an internal process and then an external process. The external process is finding the conferences, doing the networking, and following up.

We are blessed. We are doing this in the era of unlimited internet information. Between the internet and the telephone you can find out pretty much everything you need to know short of actually doing something. Even then you can probably make the connections to put yourself in a volunteer position. There are so many ways of establishing options for the future. Sometimes people come into coaching simply because they need help narrowing down their options. They may feel overwhelmed and need help coming up with a strategy.

Q. Have you written a book yet?
A. I've actually got a manuscript. I don't put enormous amounts of emphasis on it. It's a fabulous platform builder if you want to get into something, but it is actually one of the most difficult ways to make money. As soon as I have some opening

DR. PHILIPPA KENNEALY

in my time, I go back to my book. I have a rough manuscript written about the journey, but it is not my biggest money maker, and I have to keep my eye on the ball with my business.

Q. Any slogans to live by?
A. I always think my gravestone should say: "She was an enthusiastic woman." I think that is a word that characterizes me well.

Q. Enthusiastic woman. That fits you, having met you in person. You definitely have the aura and energy circulating there for sure.
A. I have two mantras that keep me going. One is, "There are two lasting bequests we can give our children: one is roots, the other is wings." Whether it is children or clients, it doesn't really matter. To me that is deeply important.

This is my other favorite by Henry Miller, "The aim of life is to live and to live means to be aware, joyously, drunkenly, serenely, divinely aware." To me, those are the two sayings that encapsulate everything that I care about. I certainly don't walk around like that all the time.

Q. Those are great. Anything else you care to add?
A. You have a question here that I think is an important one. How have your family and friends reacted to your transformation? Your own identify is carefully crafted. It takes many, many years to evolve and it become a deeply ingrained part of who we are. It is how the world sees us. In many ways it is also how our spouses view us. There is a pride in being married to a physician. I think there is a lot at stake for not only the physician, but also for the others around him.

Sometimes the toughest part of internal and external work that one has to do is around moving on to an alternative ca-

THE ENTREPRENEURIAL MD

reer. It is interesting because people look at me and say, 'What do you do?' I say, 'I used to be a physician and now I'm a coach.' My husband always looks at me and says, 'You are still a physician.' He doesn't want me to lose that identity. He's right, I'm still a physician and you can never take the MD away from my name. But I have moved on in my identity. I am not a physician. I am a physician coach and I am a mom. I have been able to do the work to broaden my identity and detach myself from the close ties of physician identity. But, it affects a lot of people and you have to be aware of that.

Believe me it took some work. It took a lot of reflection and digging into what's really important to me. If my whole life is wrapped up in my physician identity, then I am in trouble. I need to be bigger than that. Bear in mind that I went to a six year medical school and I started at the age of 18, so I graduated in 1978 in South Africa.

Q. I graduated in 1974 so I am familiar with how things have changed. Being a physician is not as dynamic as it was before. I think we need to go into these other areas and explore, that's why I'm just enjoying having a very open mind and learning from people. Do you have any other advice for physicians contemplating change besides your internal/ external process?

A. If you think it's going to make you a well-rounded person, a more fulfilled person, then go for it. Don't let your choices be ruled by fear. Too many of our choices are driven by fear. We react to our fear instead of embracing the challenge. The people that have the most fun and are most successful are those who look their fear in the face and said, "I'm going for it anyway!" These are not fearless people. None of us are fearless.

I always do what I call the death bed test. This clearly applies to me when I'm in my decision-making phase. For example, I

Dr. Philippa Kennealy

101

got to my mid-forties without having any children. That was the agreed upon deal of my marriage. We weren't going to have any children, because my husband already had three from a previous marriage. I woke up one day and realized this was somebody else's choice, not mine. So, at the same time I was giving birth to my coaching company, I was physically giving birth to a child in my late forties. I had to stare my fear in the face. I greatly feared losing a marriage I cared very much about. My husband and I got pretty upset with each other for a while, but now we are gloriously happy with one another again. So, be willing to acknowledge that while there is fear, it shouldn't be the decision-maker in your life.

THE ENTREPRENEURIAL MD

12

"I find a career coach must understand the ultimate goals of each student or physician he/she is working with. I try to approach the problem with a short-term, medium-term and long-term strategy. It is so rewarding when I'm able to help them succeed in their own transition."

Dr. Joseph Kim, Physician Technologist

Dr. Joseph Kim is a physician technologist who has a passion to leverage health information technology to improve public health. Dr. Kim is the founder of NonClinicalJobs.com and the Society of Physicians with Non-Clinical Careers (SPNCC). He is also an active social media specialist and he blogs about non-clinical medical jobs, medicine and technology, medical smart-phones, and mobile computing. Joe studied engineering from MIT, received an MD from the University of Arkansas College of Medicine, and received an MPH from UMass Amherst School of Public Health.

Q. Why did you become a physician? What were you looking for?

A. I went into medicine just like a lot of other people, hoping to help others. My intent was to go into biomedical engineering, but as I learned more about the clinical sciences, especially those related to cancer research, I felt I could contribute more by becoming a physician. That became my driving motivator.

Q. So, you graduated from college as a pre-med engineering student? Did you ever consider practicing medicine?

A. Yes, I went to medical school right after college, with the plan of practicing medicine. But, in medical school I really struggled with which specialty to pursue. I applied for both internal medicine and pediatrics residencies. I got accepted into an internal medicine program.

Q. When did it finally click that you needed to leave the practice of medicine?

A. There were a lot of personal things going on. I found the stress of constantly dealing with chronic disease, turned me into a person that I didn't like seeing in the mirror. It was after two years of residency that I decided I needed to take time off. It was then that I decided that it was time to look for other opportunities.

Q. How was your transition journey to a new career?

A. The transition was a learning experience for me. Up to that point I had known several clinicians who had decided to leave clinical practice, but I had never sat down and talked with them. So, when it was time for me to make a decision, I didn't know exactly what my options were. I did a job search and I spoke with a few people to explore my options and opportunities, but that was really not helpful. I went to my next job because that was where the opportunity presented itself, as opposed to doing any real research or seriously trying to map out my career. I applied for jobs online. I found health information technology companies who were doing some interesting things on the internet. That really interested me, and I felt that with my background in technology and healthcare would be a good fit for that type of organiza-

PHYSICIAN TECHNOLOGIST

tion. So I went to work for a company that has since been acquired by United Health. It was a steep learning curve, a real learning experience.

Q. How would you describe your present career right now?

A. I've been in the continuing medical education or CME, industry for the last five years. I enjoy it and I've learned a lot about this particular industry. Through my website NonClinicalJobs.com and through networking with other clinicians who have left clinical medicine, I've gained a much richer understanding of what career opportunities are out there. Over the years, as I went through interviews, I learned more and more about the many types of opportunities out there in different industries. That was really what caused me to start blogging on NonClinicaJobs.com, to provide a resource for medical students and clinicians who are at a point in their lives where they are contemplating what their options are if they decide to leave clinical medicine. Since I saw no solid resources on the web, I decided to create my own.

Now I feel I have an excellent understanding of many different career opportunities and options related to physicians at all levels in their professional career. I also have a better understanding of where I'm headed in my own career. Over the last few years, I've developed several parallel careers outside of my day job. I am doing a lot of work in the evenings and on weekends, and I have become an entrepreneur in several different areas. That's where I am now. I'm planning to apply to business school to get an MBA, and then probably continue with my entrepreneurial pursuits.

Q. It sounds like you are passionate about helping others to make the transition?

A. Right. The NonClinicalJobs.com website initially started out as a free blog. I wasn't making any money off of it. I wasn't advertising. It was just stories and antidotes that I had picked up along the way, and stories from other people. Over time

DR. JOSEPH KIM

I realized that traffic to my site was growing. I was receiving more and more emails, with people asking very specific questions and looking for advice. I figured there was a solid business opportunity here, not only in helping med students and physicians, but also to make this a premiere resource. I thought there would be revenue opportunities as well as far as advertising and other things along those lines.

In the spring of 2009 I took my website to a whole new level. I invested a little bit of my own money into it, and started advertising and building partnerships for advertising. I also started offering a more formal career-coaching service for physicians and others who were seeking what I would call concierge-level coaching. That has taken off. The traffic has continued to grow, and I continue to network with people who are very well connected.

Through my blog I cover major medical meetings that resonate with clinicians who want to leave clinical medicine. A few weeks ago I attended the Association of Joint MD and MBA programs. I covered their conference through a blog post on my site. Through that experience I got to know the leaders of that association as well as some of their faculty.

At the end of this month I'm going to attend the American College of Physician Executives. I hope to cover portions of that meeting. My coverage of that conference is going to be sponsored by an electronic health records company. A few months ago I covered the HIMS: Health Information Management Society, Business and Society. That was not about non-clinical jobs, but about medicine and technology blogs. So, the blogging business has really taken off for me. It has become this second career that generates a substantial amount of revenue, and it continues to grow every month.

As far as NonClinicalJobs.com, that continues to gain more momentum every month as well. In terms of helping physi-

PHYSICIAN TECHNOLOGIST

cians, I try to provide a resource for them. I also recognize that I don't have the time to personally coach each of them. That is why I have a taped service. For everyone else, I try to answer their questions the best that I can through email. I also refer them to people or resources as I am able to. I am actively involved in an online forum called the Student-Doctor Network. I am a volunteer advisor there where I answer lots of questions related to non-clinical careers and things on the business end.

Q. This is for medical students?
A. The Student-Doctor Network is predominately students and residents, but there are occasionally physicians who go to that website. It is a website that has a tremendous amount of traffic and a high volume of activity. I would say at least once a week I get a question there. By email I would say I get a handful a week from people who have questions about non-clinical careers. I try to answer them to the best of my ability given the time that I have.

Q. It seems there are a number of med students who are thinking about this early on, even before they get their degree?
A. Yes, and I think that trend is evolving. For instance, there are several cultures, like the Asian-American culture, where there is so much parental pressure to go into medicine. I personally know a lot of people who were exactly in that situation, and at the end of the day they really don't want to practice medicine. I can relate with them culturally.

I also recognize that a lot of medical students enter med school because they want to help people. And when they start seeing the business aspects and the challenges associated with delivering healthcare in this country, many of them become cynical. They realize that they aren't going to enjoy this profession.

There are a variety of reasons why people choose to leave

DR. JOSEPH KIM

medicine. Then you have your other group who are more business-focused. They are in those joint MD/MBA programs. They want to work in venture capital or investment banking, and have no interest in residency. I intersect with those people minimally, because they seem to know what they want, and they have the business know-how to get there.

It's really the people who went into medicine not anticipating that they weren't going to practice medicine. They find themselves stuck, because they have so much debt, and they really don't know what to do. They don't have access to resources like other medical students for proper guidance. These people are really hungry for information. They are the ones who are constantly coming to my site, asking questions, participating in discussions and become very involved.

Q. Do you see this trend continuing?

A. I conducted a survey a few weeks ago on my website. Among my membership network of over 1400 physicians, I asked: "Given the recent healthcare reform, are you more likely to leave medicine? Has this new law made any impact on your decision?"

I was reflecting on a survey conducted back in December by the Medicus Firm and published in the New England Journal of Medicine. They found that 30% of physicians were seriously thinking that they would now leave clinical medicine or retire before 2014.

I wanted to confirm that with my readers, so I conducted my own survey. About a third of them agreed with that previous survey. Another third of my readers have already made a transition or are in the process of making it, so the law really didn't have any impact on them. And, I would say a good 20-30% said, "I'm still not sure yet. I don't know enough about the bill. I don't really know how that is going to affect my practice."

So, I see the shift occurring. I think in this country, people are really going to be effected by healthcare reform, depending on how all of that gets rolled out. I think over the next few years we will start to see a trend of physicians choosing to leave medicine.

I've written about this quite a few times on my site, where I quote various studies conducted by different firms. The Medicus Firm is a physician placement, executive recruiting firm, but there are several other sources of survey data that seem to confirm this same attitude. Even on the physician networking sites like Sermo, these types of discussions are occurring. It is troubling because already we have a physician shortage in our country. We are forecasting that we are going to have this major shortage. Now with the passage of the reform bill, people either leave medicine or they change their practice model to exclude the public option in these government sponsored health plans. I think we may find ourselves in a much worse situation than we were pre-healthcare reform. I don't know how it's going to unfold, but I agree with you, it is troubling. I think the system in our country really needs to think about how to go about making some positive changes in this area.

Q. So your service becomes more valuable as the passing years reveal more physicians needing to make the transition?

A. Yeah, I hope so. Right now I'm trying to collaborate with other people to provide these types of services, because I'm at a saturation point, and can't keep up with the volume. I've got a day job and a family and I'm trying to find some work-life-balance. I've been doing career coaching informally for quite awhile and now formally for about a year. I'm still trying to figure out if it is a service I'm going to grow myself, or if I'm going to bring on other people to outsource it. In terms of the website and the free information there, I definitely plan

Dr. Joseph Kim

to continue to grow that.

Q. Is there anything else you would like to say?

A. I know the needs of the people that I have worked with individually are specific to their career ambitions and pursuits. I find a career coach must understand the ultimate goals of each student or physician he/she is working with. I try to approach the problem with a short-term, medium-term and long-term strategy. It is so rewarding when I'm able to help them succeed in their own transition. In the last couple months several of my clients have made successful transitions. My hope is that they transition into something they are going to truly enjoy, as opposed to simply believing that the grass is greener on the other side. Sometimes, when they are too desperate to escape from healthcare, they land in some corporate position where they are even more miserable than before.

What I try to do is outline all the possible outcomes and make sure they have thought through the many consequences of this decision, so that they are not more dissatisfied or miserable than before. If they are, I feel I have done them a disservice.

It is essential to do a lot of exploration ahead of time. I help my clients think through where they want to go, what they ultimately want to do, and what their career goals are. When people are in transition mode, they really don't know what to do, or where to go, partially because they don't know what their options are. Once they get a clearer understanding of what they can do, as well as what steps are needed to get there, they start formulating their own long-term plan, and then work backward from there.

PHYSICIAN TECHNOLOGIST

13

"It amazes me how many opportunities are out there for doctors, and how little doctors know about these opportunities. There are thousands of jobs in all different areas. MDs often sell themselves short and don't realize they have skills that translate far beyond the clinical practice."

Dr. Michael McLaughlin, Author and Co-Founder

Michael J. McLaughlin, MD is co-founder of Peloton Advantage (www.pelotonadvantage.com), a medical communications company focused on publication planning and content development. He received degrees from Harvard College and Columbia University's College of Physicians and Surgeons. After four years as a plastic surgeon and hand specialist, he networked through a career change into medical communications. He then rose from Associate Medical Director to Sr. VP, Chief Scientific Officer within four years. Dr. McLaughlin founded Physician Renaissance Network (www.PRNresource.com), a free information and networking service for doctors with non-clinical careers and interests. He wrote the book <u>Do You Feel Like You Wasted All That Training? Questions from Doctors Considering a Career Change</u>. In 2009 he was selected in the category of Change Agents as one of the 100 Most Inspiring People in the life sciences industry by PharmaVOICE.

Q. When and why did you decide to become a doctor?
A. I decided to become a doctor around age 17. I was still in high school. At that time I decided that I wanted to be a heart surgeon. More specifically, a transplant surgeon. So, for the next several years, through high school, college, and all the way through medical school, I was striving towards accomplishing that goal. For me it was always the goal of becoming a surgeon, as early as my junior year of high school.

Q. Wow! What happened? How did that dream sour for you?
A. A few different things. When you're 17 years old, you can't anticipate what may happen latter in your life. It's hard for any high school student to figure out what they want to do. I got married after the end of medical school, and I think that started to change my perspective a little bit.

Then, during my internship, I got my first real experience with being a doctor. Up to that point, I hadn't had any close interaction with other physicians, so I got a better understanding of what their lives are like. As I began my internship, still set on becoming a cardiac transplant surgeon, I started to get a good look at that lifestyle, day to day. The work then became less appealing to me, partly because some of the novelty of it all had started to wear off. I also started to reassess what type of life I wanted to live. I realized I didn't want to be at the hospital twenty-four hours a day. It was important for me to have a family, and be involved in other activities as well.

AUTHOR AND CO-FOUDNER

I started to reassess what I wanted to do. During my residency I ran into some stumbling blocks, because I realized I didn't want to be a cardiac surgeon anymore. I obviously had a better understanding of what it was like to be a general surgeon. That left me with an interesting predicament. I was completing a surgery program and certain at that point that I didn't want to do surgery.

Luckily, I got some exposure to different types of surgery, and became very interested in hand surgery. There are three different ways to get into hand surgery, either through a general surgery residency, orthopedics, or plastic surgery. At Columbia, I was lucky enough to combine these, so that in five years I could complete my plastic surgery residency, and then go on to a hand surgery fellowship.

I still wasn't 100% sure I would be satisfied as a hand surgeon, but I was so busy doing my training that I really had no time to even get out of the hospital, let alone sort through these challenging issues in my life and explore other career opportunities. So, when I finished all of my training, I remember the day I was signing my contract to start my career as a hand surgeon, I was still wondering whether I'd be happy. It didn't take too long for me to realize that it wasn't the right career for me.

Q. Seriously? You signed the contract and then walked away?
A. It's a very tough thing to do. I decided at that point that I had to give it a shot, because I had spent the last fourteen years in training for that career. I didn't want to abandon it immediately. But after only two years, I became convinced that I no longer wanted to be in clinical practice as a hand surgeon. That left me with an interesting predicament because as far as I knew at the time, there was absolutely nothing else that I could do with my training.

The only thing I knew was clinical practice, or some type of research or academic teaching position. Other than that, I really hadn't had any exposure to anything else. As I came to the realization that I didn't want to be a hand surgeon, I had absolutely no idea what I wanted to try next. In fact, I didn't think there was anything else I could do. I was extremely demoralized at that point.

It took me about two years to explore my career options. This was back in 2001. There were no textbooks telling me what my options were. The internet options that I was able to find at that time were very limited and fragmented. There was very little written on the subject in general. And for a doctor who has trained my whole life, reading books and articles and learning from my peers, there was really no way for me to learn very efficiently what my options were.

Luckily I had a relative who had left medicine very early in his career and gone on to start a successful business, followed by multiple entrepreneurial endeavors that were also successful. He spent the next two years coaching me through my options, how to prioritize what I wanted to do and which options were best for me, and then how to pursue a new career outside of clinical practice. We met every week or so throughout those two years, until I was able to make a career transition.

It wasn't until my networking and all of my research led me to the possibility of combining my two loves - medicine and writing - into a career in medical communication, that I was finally satisfied that I had found what I was looking for. Then it was immediately obvious to me that I found the solution. I realized I could go into this new career as a positive move forward, rather than escape from something I was unhappy with. That was eye-opening and very satisfying to me.

AUTHOR AND CO-FOUDNER

Q. What did you learn during your transition? Anything you can share with anyone going through a transition right now?

A. Like anything else we do as physicians, there needs to be organization to how we go about the transition process. What I was lacking when I started to think about alternative careers, was an understanding of how to organize my search. My relative, who also served as my mentor, was instrumental in teaching me how to put a methodology around the process.

In the end it came down to a series of steps. The first was introspection, where I evaluated my options, trying to decide what it was that I liked and disliked about being a hand surgeon. The next step was exploration. I began looking around at everything that was available out there. Then, I started to match that up with the results from my introspection process.

After you decide what it is you might want to do, you then need to look at your credentials to decide if you will need any further preparation. In my case, as I began looking into a career in medical communication, I realized I would need more expertise in writing. I had a good amount of experience before that point, but I knew I needed to strengthen that.

I had written several clinical articles and editorials during the course of my training. I also loved writing short stories. I've written lots of short stories over the years, and I've also written a few novel manuscripts. In my spare time I always did a lot of writing. So, for me writing was a key component in piecing together a career that made the most sense for me.

What I started to do after I decided to go into medical communications, was to begin writing on a number of different websites. I took on as many opportunities as I could and did it all for free to gain experience. I was also building my

DR. MICHAEL MCLAUGHLIN

resume as a writer. One of the advantages to writing on the web, is that I could create a CV through a number of links to my work, so someone who was interested in me can quickly look at my online portfolio.

That helped a lot. That's something I recommend to people. But first you need to know what it is you want to do, so you can prepare for it. A lot of people ask me whether or not they should get an MBA, for example. I really think it's important to first figure out what it is you would do with that MBA. It takes so much of a financial and time commitment to get that degree. I think if you have a good plan in place and getting an MBA is a part of it, then that makes sense. However, I see a lot of physicians who aren't sure what they want to do and are considering an MBA, in hopes it will somehow open up ideas and possibilities for them in the future. I think those people might end up spending a lot of money and time without necessarily reaching the end point they are looking for. That is the next step in the five part transition sequence. The fourth part is acquisition, where you begin to prepare your CV. You need to go out and interview to demonstrate your transferable skill set to a non-clinical job.

Now you need to make some decisions around your own transition. How much notice do you want to give to your current practice or current employer? How you are going to help transition your patients to the care of another doctor? What are you going to do about your certification, licensing, hospital privileges and maintaining your board status?

A lot of these things cost money, but in my case, it was important to me not to burn any bridges, especially if I wasn't sure if I would be satisfied in my next job. You always want to make sure that you have your clinical practice to fall back on if you need to do so.

Q. Sounds very well thought out and well organized. Something a surgeon would be capable of writing.

A. I think if you had spoken to me ten years ago, I would have seemed a lot less organized. I had to struggle through it in order to figure out a lot of this. That is why at this point I try to help other physicians, so that they don't have to spend two years figuring out how to get what they want. They can figure it out a little more efficiently and hopefully do very well as far as their selection and acquisition of a new job.

Q. Going through your own transition, what was your biggest obstacle or breakthrough?

A. I think the biggest obstacle for me was that early part, where I was afraid there wasn't anything I could do outside of clinical practice. There were a couple of doctors in my residency program who left clinical practice early. One left after our internship and one left after our second year of general surgery residency. Looking back, I think they were fortunate that they were able to figure out what it was they wanted to do with their careers much earlier than I. It took me a lot longer, because of the many hours I spent in the hospital during my residency, and the severely limited amount of time I had to sort out my other options. That was probably the biggest hurdle.

As far as my biggest breakthrough, that was the realization that I would be able to combine two passions into one career. I've always loved medicine. I still find all of the scientific and clinical aspects of medicine to be very interesting. I've always loved to write. Once I realized that I could have a career that involved both medicine and writing, that was an epiphany for me! Then it was just a matter of time to make it work.

Q. What about your future? You are a leader in the field of transitional medicine, physicians in transition. There are going to be new trends, new strategies and new discover-

Dr. Michael McLaughlin

ies. I understand there is going to be a physician shortage and a lot of that shortage is going to be from physicians transitioning out of clinical practice. What do you see in those areas?

A. In the last several years I've been involved in the topic of non-clinical careers and physician career transition. In 2004 I started a Physicians' Renaissance Network (PRN), which is a resource for doctors who are interested in non-clinical careers and activities. The doctors who are members of PRN are a mixture of physicians who are in non-clinical careers already, physicians who are in clinical practice but want to learn about career alternatives, as well a physicians who want to remain in clinical practice, but also want to learn about non-clinical jobs such as consulting or writing. Through PRN I maintain a website with a lot of information, as well as a newsletter that goes out on a monthly basis. We also offer a free members-only networking page that allows physicians to interact with each other on these topics. I think it's really important for physicians who are involved in these types of career transitions, to find each other and exchange ideas.

Back when I was getting started, nothing like this existed. I thought it was extremely important to begin offering these types of services. Now, through my website, physicians can come together and teach each other about what they do, share opportunities with each other, share best practices and learn what they've done to succeed in their careers. In the past it was just me working on the website, but now that the membership has grown significantly, I've found that the members are helping each other out in a way that has expanded far beyond what I can accomplish by myself.

One area I think is important is that pre-med students, but also those in medical school and during residency, learn about all these different options that are out there for physicians. A lot more people might be interested in going to medical school in the first place if they realized all of the fascinating things doctors can do with their degrees. This

AUTHOR AND CO-FOUDNER

then becomes particularly important for medical students and residents as they are going through their education and advanced training. PRN has a lot of medical student and resident members. They all really come in saying, "I want to find out what options are out there for me and learn more about them."

I think it would be great if medical schools taught their students about all of these options. There is still a reluctance to teach anything beyond mainstream medicine, clinical practice, research and academic education. There are many different careers physicians can pursue outside of the more traditional paths. Many physicians work in medical communication. Others work in pharmaceutical companies. Other areas such as medical informatics are becoming very substantial as the amount of physician expertise increases to move those initiatives forward.

There are physicians who work in publishing, who do legal work, physicians who work in insurance companies, and physicians who work in the financial sector. The jobs are really out there everywhere. The trick is still to connect the individual with these jobs. This is what I try to do with PRN and what I think is really important to do in the future. I think society in general benefits when the best person finds the best possible career that suits them and their skill set, and allows them to provide the most to the people around them.

Q. Is there anything else that you have a burning desire to comment on?

A. There are a couple more things I would like to add. When I was going along the track to become a physician, my entire career was moving along a very distinct linear path. But what happens when you reach a point where you want to branch out and do something different? Only then do you realize that the number of possibilities out there for you are actually limitless, and far beyond the linear path that we are

DR. MICHAEL MCLAUGHLIN

used to following.

I reached a point where I realized I didn't want to continue on the linear path I was on. I took a look around and at first found it to be a daunting proposition that I could choose anything in the world to do. But then, following the process of sorting through all of my options, I was able to move on to something different.

When I was younger I used to see a career as having a defined endpoint. When I was in clinical practice I reached at least a temporary endpoint, in which I was a practicing surgeon. I realize now that my career is actually an evolution rather then a single series of points. I am always looking for opportunities to enhance my career in various ways.

I'm currently a business owner of a company called Peloton Advantage which is a medical communications company. Even within Peloton Advantage we are always looking for ways to expand our services and the experiences that we have. That is an extremely rewarding component of being a business owner.

I am also involved in these non-clinical activities in addition to my primary career is as a business owner and I'm always looking for ways to expand my experience. Ever since 2001, when I stepped out of my linear career path, my career has really opened up as far as all of the different aspects of business and medicine that I'm exposed to.

Q. A couple of physicians have mentioned to me that medicine can become a bit boring, the same thing over and over again with no room for creativity.

A. I have one other thought for you. Back a couple of years ago when I started to explore my career opportunities, I was very frustrated. It was difficult being in a career unsuited to me, wondering if there was any way that I could ever do anything else. I felt frustrated because I had let myself down. Now that I've made my full career transition, worked through a couple of different jobs, and moved on to owning my own company, when I look back, I'm actually very satisfied that I went to medical school and became a physician. It may have taken me a bit longer than it should have to find something non-clinical to do with my degree and my career, but I definitely wouldn't be able to do what I'm doing now without first becoming a physician.

I know there are a lot of doctors out there who are frustrated in their current career and are considering a transition. They are probably also feeling frustrated and disappointed. But if they will keep their eye open for opportunities and sort through their options, hopefully they will find satisfaction through their own career transition, and then be glad of their original decision to become a doctor.

It amazes me how many opportunities are out there for doctors, and how little doctors know about these opportunities. There are thousands of jobs in all different areas. MDs often sell themselves short and don't realize they have skills that translate far beyond the clinical practice. Being a physician allows you to have various skill sets that are desirable to many different types of employers. Physicians are intelligent, hardworking, dedicated, used to working independently, and confident in what they can do. Many of them have run their own practices, so they have business skills they are not even aware of in many cases.

DR. MICHAEL MCLAUGHLIN

"There is vitality, life force, energy that is translated through you into action, and because there is only one of you, your expression is unique. If you block it, it will never exist through any other medium and be lost forever. It is not your business to determine how good or valuable it compares with other expressions, it is your business to keep the channel open."

- Martha Graham

"Make your life happy now, instead of continually battling your fears."

Dr. Ola Medhat , Physician Advisor

Dr. Ola Medhat grew up in Kansas City where she attended undergraduate and medical school. She moved to California for her residency training in Family Medicine at The University of California, Irvine. Dr. Medhat pursued her entrepreneurial passion after completing her residency by managing her own private practice for 11 years after which she decided to pursue other facets of medicine. Currently, Dr. Medhat is a Physician Advisor managing Medicare & Medicaid regulatory compliance.

Q. Why did you want to become a doctor?

A. I really enjoyed caring for others and also enjoyed math & science in school. There was also definitely an influence from my family. My father is a doctor and my mother is a nurse which helped mold my path since junior high.

Q. So what happened when you decided to leave clinical medicine? How did your family respond?

A. At first they just couldn't understand why I would want such a change especially since they have such a strong passion for the profession. I had my own private practice for eleven years. During that time I started to get very frustrated with patient care, insurance regulations and the business side of medicine. I was to the point where I just really wanted to get out of medicine completely; however, my family initially discouraged me. Then, over time, once they realized how unhappy I was in my career, they became more supportive.

Q. What significant event finally made you decide to make the switch?

A. I got really burnt out by the demanding patients, the insurance companies, the lack of reimbursement and so forth. About two years ago, I finally woke up one day and thought, "What am I doing? I need my life back. I have given my entire life to this career and the return is really not worth the sacrifice." That's when I decided to close my practice and position myself for a smooth transition. I closed my practice in 2009. I have been working in an Urgent Care facility for about one year, and just last week I was fortunate enough to land a non-clinical job with a great company called Executive Health Resources, based out of Philadelphia. I will be an advocate for my colleagues by doing case reviews for hospitals to help them comply with Medicare regulations. I am very excited that I can use my clinical knowledge and my joy for science without having to do direct patient care.

> "...realizing that we only have one chance at this life, we really need to make the best of it and do what makes us happy."

Q. Does this job require any extra training on your part?

A. Yes, the company will be training me to their specifications.

Q. Is there any advice you could give to others? What have you learned on your journey?

A. Well, first of all, make sure you are happy in whatever path you choose. Regarding the transition, it really is all about networking. I spent some time on the internet and looking at job boards without much return. I found this opportunity through a colleague.

Q. Did you ever consider using a mentor on any of the online websites?

A. I did get some career coaching from Dr. Joseph Kim. He's quite knowledgeable about the non-clinical arena. Initially, I felt very lost without any direction. I think a lot of doctors who have been practicing clinical medicine are in that same boat. We don't even know where to start. All we know is clinical medicine, so having a mentor was a tremendous help. I also attended a SEAK Conference in 2008. I was really surprised by the number of physicians wanting to transition. But everyone felt very lost, didn't know where to go and how to do it. I found Joe through the internet and he was very helpful in getting me organized, pointing me in the right direction, and offering guidance.

Q. What have you learned for yourself through this?

A. One of the major factors for me was my quality of life. That became more and more important over the last few years. When I was younger, I was so focused on becoming a doctor that I didn't really pay much attention to the rest of my life. So this transition has been really eye-opening. Just realizing that we only have one chance at this life, we really need to make the best of it and do what makes us happy. I think that was one thing I learned over the course of my career. Continuing the clinical medicine for another twenty years was just not an option for me.

Dr. Ola Medhat

Q. It sounds like you found a way to do this without much financial risk, or any outlay of money?

A. This is actually a better financial opportunity with possibility for advancement. Currently, in clinical medicine, advancement is very limited due to the high cost of overhead, etc.

Q. Any future plans? I know some of the physicians I spoke to have had a good experience working with others along the way and felt strongly about trying to stay connected. Do you see yourself staying in contact with those you have met through your own transition?

A. I think so. From my experience and the knowledge I have gained, I want to be proactive in trying to help others who want to transition as well. Once I get settled, I will probably contact some of the doctors I met along my journey to see how they are doing and how I might be able to assist them.

My advice to anybody considering a change would be to go after your passion. Make your life happy now, instead of continually battling your fears.

PHYSICIAN ADVISOR

15

"I want to leave this world a little bit better, and leave things behind that will continue on long beyond my time."
Dr. Rita Meek, Medical Director

Let's follow Trailblazer Rita Meek, MD on her ever transitioning career path as she continues to lead others in directions never taken before. As she cuts through the underbrush and knocks barriers out of the way she leaves a path that others can follow and improve their lives. When she faces a fork in the path intuition, passion, and doing the right thing for the patient lead her to the correct choice. Along the way she discovers hidden treasures which she will share with you.

BACKGROUND
Rita grew up in the Washington DC area, more specifically in a Maryland suburb of DC. She attended NYU as undergraduate, and then continued on to graduate school at the University of Pennsylvania. She finally attended medical school at George Washington University.

INTERVIEW
Q. When did you know that you wanted to be a physician?
A. I probably knew I wanted to be a physician early in the process, but it did not even seem like a possibility, since I didn't have the financial resources. So I went to graduate school which I thought was a fine alternative.

When I was a graduate student in physiology at the University of Pennsylvania, they sent us with the medical students to take classes at the Children's Hospital. One day I was standing in the lobby of the children's hospital in Philadelphia and I had this kind of realization — I don't know what you call it; an epiphany or whatever, though it sounds a little high-fluting – but all the sudden I had this feeling and this sense that that is what I was supposed to do.

I talked to my then fiancée and decided that somehow we would make that work. I quit graduate school shortly thereafter even though people in the graduate program who kept saying, "You can and get a master's – only one more semester and you will get a masters," and I said, "But I didn't want a masters. I was never going to do anything with this and I am not going to do that. I was moving on and I was going to do something else that I want to do." So I left and applied to medical school.

I started medical school in the fall, and then I tried to maintain an open mind about what I would do and what I was going to specialize in. I liked everything and I did well. But about half way through the third year of medical school I would get into the car on the morning of the first day of whatever rotation and I would think, "You know, there are 30 lucky people starting at Children's this morning," as I headed out to psychiatry or OBGYN or surgery or whatever it was. About three-quarters through the year I thought, "You know, there is probably a message there." So at that point I decided that I liked everything, but that was probably where I needed to be. I never looked back from that decision.

Q. So you became a pediatrician?
A. Yes.

Q. You started your career path as a grad student in physiology and now you are traveling on your path as a pediatrician. What's next?
A. Well, it was another kind of event, like the first event. I am guided by these moments where I really have this sense that there is a fork in the path and this is the path I am suppose to take. At that time, I was a second year pediatric resident ro-

MEDICAL DIRECTOR

tating through 2 months at a community hospital. My mother had a surgical procedure while I was doing my second year pediatric rotation there. I was pretty sure that she had some type of uterine cancer.

The GYN called me after the surgery and he told me everything was fine and everything was great. Then he called me a couple of days later and said, "Well, the pap is back and your mother has an adenocarcinoma of the uterus. I said, "Okay." Then he didn't say anything, so I said, "So what are the next steps?" He said, "Well, I am going to tell her everything is fine and when she comes for her checkup, then I am going to tell her that we only need to do a little bit of radiation just to make sure that everything stays fine."

Now in 2010; I'm not 100% sure it was shocking in 1976, but I said – here I was like 25 and here this guy was like late 50's and clearly a very experienced GYN, not somebody in their second year of residency – and I said, "Well actually doctor, that is not going to be okay," which, as I look back, I think, "What was I thinking," but I said that and I said, "Because actually, my parents know that I am here and really what you are asking me to do is to collude with you into telling her that everything is fine and then later telling her that everything really is not fine. My parents know that I am here and that I would have checked things out, so I really can't do that, because really what you are asking me to do is lie to my parents and I can't do that." Then he didn't say anything and then he said, "Well, if you feel that way about it, you go talk to her and tell her and I will be there in the morning." I said, "Well, actually doctor, let me remind you that I am the daughter and you are the doctor. Your job is to tell her and my job is to support my parents. I will go

> **"...reinvent yourself every ten years because it keeps you young, keeps you engaged, and keeps you interesting..."**

with you or I will follow you, but I am not doing your work for you." Probably he did not know what had transpired or who this person was on the other end of the phone, but I remember hanging up the phone being so angry. This was in the mid '70's when it was okay not to tell people what was wrong with them but it really wasn't okay with me, and I said to myself, "If this is the way that people treat people who have cancer, I can do a better job."

Q. So that was the turning point in your decision to leave pediatrics?

A. Well I did not leave pediatrics altogether but rather I chose to specialize in Pediatric Heme-Onc. This just showed me a path that I felt in my heart was the right path.

Q. Had you had any notion of Heme-Onc before that, or was it this only experience?

A. It certainly wasn't something that I was fixed upon. I had kind of kept my options open realizing that you change your opinion as you get exposed to more and more things. I certainly didn't go to medical school thinking that I would wind up as a pediatric oncologist.

Q. So were there things – being a pediatrician- that you just did not like and sort of moved away from them to get into this specialty?

A. What I felt I needed, was more balance in my career. The fork in the path was Heme-Onc which provided the combination of sick kids that I could really make a difference for in the management and having patients and families that I had a long-term relationship with. I needed both of these elements to fuel my passion.

Q. What an enchanting, ever-evolving, dynamic career path you have created. The suspense is killing me. What's next?

A. What happened was by the time, oh 1998 or something like that, as Division Chief of Pediatric Heme-Onc, I was running a program that had about 30 people reporting to me and I decided that I didn't know much about management and that I needed some kind of training in how to better manage people. This knowledge would give me more understanding of interpersonal dynamics and how to manage people and how to work collaboratively with people to move towards a vision or make things happen. I decided to get this very odd degree called the Master's of Science in Organization Development, which is not a typical degree for a physician. My boss encouraged me because I was looking for something else and I was just not sure what the path was. I did that and in that process I heard about this degree and it was at American University in Washington.

Washington is about 2 hours south of Delaware – Washington D.C. It was an executive master's, which means it was a Friday, Saturday, and Sunday once a month. I decided that was doable. I headed off on this journey, which in retrospect was probably a good thing for me. It certainly stretched me in ways and it has nothing to do with physicians. Would you believe that in the 15-20 years of running this course there had never been a physician in the class? People just could not believe that there was a physician who was doing this. That was actually good for me to have to understand how not everybody sees the world as physicians do. That was an important thing because I had lived such an insular life for such a long time, in terms of dealing with people who kind of lived and breathed medicine, that to meet somebody who was a realtor and having to be doing a project with them, let's say, or someone who was a banker, was a very different way of learning that my way wasn't necessarily the only right way, except for me.

Q. Can you clarify for me? You were doing this as the hospital medical director?

A. No, not yet. I was still the division chief for Heme-Onc. Then after I finished this degree – and I was still the division chief for Heme-Onc – then the hospital decided it wanted a medical director. By that time I had been there for a long time; I had been the president of the medical staff, I had done a lot of different things, and I think at that point people figured that I probably could do this job and do a good job so they offered me the position as the hospital medical director which was really a new position because nobody had ever done it before as a focus.

Q. So hopefully you didn't encounter too many obstacles since you knew everybody there.

A. Well, the obstacles were unbelievable, but I would say that being a hospital medical director, in many ways, is like herding cats. You have everybody who is independent and they think they know the right way to get something done and you have 400 people. I had no direct authority over anybody as the hospital medical director; in this particular organization which is set up in a very unusual structure, no body reported to me – the department chairs didn't report to me, nobody reported to me, so I was kind of out there trying to accomplish things without any direct authority over anybody.

I remained division chief for about another year to two years and then I just said, "I can't do this and do a good job; I can't do a good job in both jobs." The hospital job needed structure – I had made a commitment that I was going to do that. I felt that was the place where I could really make a difference, so I gave up being the division chief of Heme-Onc. And I took on the opportunity to be the hospital medical director and put a lot of structure in place – infrastructure in place – that helped the medical staff have not policies for policies stake, but a clear understanding of what the expectations were and how to move in the system and very committed to patient safety and quality, so very much into "we have to do it this way because it's the right thing to do for the children," and trying to make sure that the doctors understand the plan – I saw myself as a bridge.

MEDICAL DIRECTOR

When I was with the administration, I needed to be the physician who was representing the physicians; when I was with the physicians, I needed to be the administrator who was bringing them the information that they needed to know in order to function correctly in the hospital. It was really very much of a dual hat kind of role and it would float back and forth very quickly, but I worked very hard to make sure that both sides saw me as being a reasonable conveyer of news.

It was kind of a job like that, which was very interesting, and I really think that I took the job to certainly a different level than it was when I inherited it, which was centrally that nobody had done much of anything with it, so by the end of doing that, I think the physicians had much more of a clear voice in this organization. I paved the way for a lot of other things to happen – for women, for...just a number of things. I also developed an "open door" policy, so the physicians could drop in any time. So they would come and the reason that I thought that was positive is they would come knowing that I would listen to what they had to say and try to either help them address it or take their concern up to somebody else.

I was handed the opportunity to write and institute peer review for our organization, so I wrote a peer-review policy after lots of iterations and then started a peer review committee which I chaired for four years – from its inception, so maybe six years – so I designed peer review, not in a vacuum, but basically I listened collaborative and went forward and it doesn't look exactly the same way when I finished it, but it is a very robust peer-review program and I still sit on that committee. I think – I feel that I made a tremendous contribution to the organization and I am not the – I don't know how to say this – just because someone tells me that isn't going to be how that's going to be, that's not enough for me to stop. So, I think the physicians got their voice in the room in a way

DR. RITA MEEK

they had never before.

Q. You were able to transition to your newer careers in a large part by following intuition and passion?

A. It's true and I should just briefly tell you about my current path, or what I am doing now, because I think it's just another example of that. I am now the division chief for a new division, and just like I started, I started being the only member of the division and I am ending up as the only member of the division, which is called "Transition of Care." It is focusing on the needs of young adults with special health care needs when they leave pediatrics and move into the adult medical environment.

Q. What age group is that?

A. That is probably anybody from 18 to 21, in our organization. We are not allowed to take care of anybody beyond the age of 21; that's the thing under which we operate. It's complicated, but the bottom line is my current job is to try to see how I can improve that process for patients, their families, the doctors who are receiving them, the doctors who need to let them go – all of those areas need to kind of move in a certain direction in order to have this population of people have the best chance for being successfully integrated into the adult world and be able to be the most that they are capable of being.

The population that perhaps is the most affected by this is young adults with cerebral palsy and mental retardation. They have the biggest problem in finding all of the sub-specialty care they need.

Q. I am getting a visual here – I don't have the complete thing yet – but I have you skipping through the clouds dressed in flowing gowns and embracing the clouds and the people living there. You are just following your passion and your

MEDICAL DIRECTOR

intuition and you have movement and you leave everything a little bit better than how you found it. It's a fantastic job and you are a fantastic person in the way you convey these energies.

A. Well, I have a lot of energy – maybe a little less than I did 30 years ago when I started oncology here – but I am somebody who can have a vision. That's my greatest strength, I think, is I really can have a clear vision of where I think we need to go and then the challenge is to get people to jump on with me. We can do this – we can do this together if we all believe. It's a little bit like Tinkerbelle! [Laughing] "Clap your hands if you believe!"

Q. **Opportunity and resultant growth have been so important for you, why?**

A. Opportunity for growth for me, but to push the envelope in a way that benefits other people, particularly children, which – of course- is the motivation that I have, but it's never because I wanted to be the hospital medical director and I grew up because that's what I wanted to do and I wanted the title, and I wanted to the be the CEO – that was not part of this at all. It was just that I could make a difference for the kids in this state if I am the hospital medical director of the children's hospital. I can help people move this into a better – to do better care for children in this state, better quality, patient safety, support the physicians – I can help do that. It was the same thing with transition. I don't know anything about transition except that I probably know more than anybody else around here, so I am learning as I go.

Q. **Your career defines the successful fulfilled passionate physician in transition.**

A. That's right – that's why I thought I would want to end with that. I feel like I have just been in transition the whole time.

Q. **Do you do any speaking?**

A. I do speaking, sure. I am always happy – I mean, not always happy to speak, but if someone wants to hear something I have to say, I am happy to speak. I have lectured. As part of this, we have academic appointments at Jefferson, so I have been involved with teaching my whole time.

I am very interested in supporting physicians through malpractice. That is a whole different sideline that I have worked on.

I have been sued three times – and I found one case to be just so personally devastating and I thought the medical system did such a terrible job of supporting a physician going through this. I just thought, "Well, the good that came out of this is that I have to help physicians – I have to help the system do a better job of supporting physicians." That is something that I have been involved with. We did a movie, a video, of four senior physicians, including myself, talking about their malpractice experience and a number of talks about the impact of malpractice on physicians. I talk once a year at the law school to kind of talk about what malpractice is from a physician's standpoint as opposed to a lawyer's standpoint – how we view this in such a different way. So, that's something else that I am interested in and have done a fair amount of work in. That's, I think, all that I can think of to tell you!

Q. What advice do you have for other physicians who are contemplating changing their career, stepping out of medicine and going forward?

A. It's making sure you have what you need. Make sure you are not just blindly stepping off. I will tell you one thing – I don't know if this is the right answer or not – but at every step along the way, I have said to myself, "What's the worst thing that can happen?" The worst thing that can happen is I don't have a job. If they don't like me as the hospital medical director and they fire me, oh well – I will be looking for a job as a pediatrician for about four minutes. I mean, so it is a little bit like "Just do it." Just do it because you have something to fall back on. As long as you are willing to kind of land not completely on your feet, but enough that you can get by, then do it.

Q. Are there any certain slogans you live by or are always telling people?

A. One thing would be to reinvent yourself every ten years because it keeps you young, keeps you engaged, keeps you interesting and interested, and it gives room for other people to build on the foundation that you have laid. Do the right thing for the children and whatever choice you make will ultimately turn out to be the right one." So, I think those are two for me that are good things to live by.

Q. How would you like to be remembered?

A. As having made a difference in people's lives. I can only tell you how I have had that and maybe not in grandiose terms, but leaving the world a little bit better and leaving things behind me that will continue on long beyond my time. I won this award once in Delaware called the trailblazer award and it's an award given to a woman in Delaware who has led in a direction that has not been taken before.

Q. So you would like to be remembered as a trailblazer?

A. Yes, I guess that's me.

DR. RITA MEEK

Rita's career transition in summary

Career path: Grad student, med student, general pediatrician, Pediatric Oncology specialist, Division Chief of Oncology, Hospital Medical Director (both jobs at same time), Hospital Medical Director, Founder of "Transition of Care" division (current)

Turning Points, Events, Aha! Moments

- Lobby of children's hospital = go to medical school
- Driving car 3rd year med school = go into peds
- Mother's Cancer = go into oncology subspecialty
- Division Chief of Oncology (needed more balance in life— needed more understanding of interpersonal dynamics and how to manage people to work collaboratively with people to make things happen..) = Needed more training = Master's of Science in Organization Development (an executive Master's degree.)
- Pediatric patients needed better follow-up as they reached 18 years of age and moved into the adult medical environment = Improved this process for the patient by starting a division of "Transition of Care."

Treasures

- Reinvent yourself every 10 years.
- Just do the right thing for the children (patient or client) and it will all work out.
- Don't ignore intuition, passion and your heart when facing forks in your path.
- Be a Trailblazer. Get through the underbrush and knock the barriers out of the way so that when you look back there is a path that others can follow.

MEDICAL DIRECTOR

138

"I had a degree from a prestigious college, had been accepted to my top residency program, had a bright future with a decent salary and job security waiting for me, and all I felt was angry and afraid. I didn't want what came with it, the practice of medicine."
Dr. Michelle Mudge-Riley, The Doctor's Doctor

DR. MICHELLE MUDGE-RILEY

Dr. Mudge-Riley successfully made the transition from clinical practice to non-direct clinical work and now works as a consultant for brokerage firms and large employers in Wellness and Health Promotion in Richmond, Virginia. She has spent the past seven years advising other doctors on how to enhance their career and on transitioning to a non-clinical career through Physicians Helping Physicians under Integrate Health For Results, LLC. She has worked with thousands of doctors located in various locations throughout the United States.

Dr. Mudge-Riley works on an individual basis with each client to help with such things as:

- Finding resources and options for clinical or non-clinical work

- Salary considerations
- CV/resume assistance (including cover letter)
- Assistance with "elevator pitch"
- Leveraging social media
- Assistance with personal reflection and direction
- Personal development plan, goals and objectives
- Networking assistance
- Finding ways to turn ideas into money

Dr. Mudge-Riley received her medical degree from Des Moines University Osteopathic Medical School and her Masters Degree in Health Administration from Virginia Commonwealth University. She completed a medical internship at Virginia Commonwealth University Hospital System (VCUHS) and a business residency under the CEO of the same hospital system. She has been directly responsible for planning, implementation, communication, and evaluation of programs involving healthcare wellness, safety, and quality within a variety of industries.

Michelle has conducted seminars on topics related to change management, motivation, wellness and health education. She has also been published in a variety of journals including Physicians Practice Magazine and The D.O.

An avid runner and biker, she was the fourth woman to cross the finish line at the Richmond Marathon in 2006 and has completed more than 20 marathons and half marathons.

Q. Why did you become a physician?
A. Who wouldn't after wanting to my entire life? I used to read *The Mayo Clinic Handbook* for fun when I was twelve! I loved learning about different diseases and how the body worked. I've always been fascinated with medicine and I'm a good student, at least I can memorize like nobody's business. I once memorized my entire AP history textbook! Obviously that led to good grades and admission to a top college. My father was so supportive of my decision to go into medicine.

THE DOCTOR'S DOCTOR

Once I was in college, I set my sights on getting into medical school on my first try. I knew it wouldn't be easy. I tried to maximize my chances of success by writing to 50 medical doctors nationwide, ones I found listed in a book at my college library. I asked them why they had decided to become a doctor, and what advice they had for me. Sure enough, I got into medical school on my first try!

Q. What happened in medical school?

A. My first two years of medical school were pure bliss. But uncertainty about my future career choice began in my third year, when we started clinical rotations on the wards. I was such a novice. I knew basically nothing about day-to-day patient care. But instead of learning all the clinical aspects of medicine from the doctors, I began to pick up on a lot of unhappiness among all of the specialties.

Most of them felt like they were wasting away at their jobs. They were either too busy or bored. That was my first glimpse of doctors who had completed their training, and now what? They were burned out from the journey or bored with the repetition of their specialty. Some were bitter about the environment or the lack of control in their lives. They muttered about missing the past ten to fifteen years of their own lives, and that of their families. And they saw no end in sight.

I also started to recognize certain similar symptoms of those bored or burned out doctors in myself. Symptoms like unrealistic expectations, unreasonable anger at various situations, and periods of profound sadness. I stopped reaching out to my friends and family. I no longer felt capable or empowered to be successful at anything.

I had a degree from a prestigious college, had been accepted to my top residency program, had a bright future with a decent salary and job security waiting for me, and all I felt was

141

angry and afraid. I didn't want what came with it, the practice of medicine. I saw the next ten years of my life flying by, and I knew I wouldn't be able to enjoy them. I was losing touch with what was meaningful and satisfying in my life.

What were those things I felt I was missing out on? They were things like having time to sit with a friend and talk about life while drinking a latte, or going on a run or joining an adult soccer league. Things like reading a novel purely for pleasure or sleeping through the night for a week straight without being called out. They were things like having oatmeal with my fiancé, and then sitting out on the deck as the morning sun shone through the trees. Yes, they were little things, but to me, they were what made me happy, satisfied and fulfilled in life.

Q. How did you decide to leave clinical medicine?

A. This was a very confusing time for me. I felt a lot of shame and fear and wondered about my identity, which was all tied up with becoming a doctor. My family didn't know what to do when I voiced my discontent. They were so proud of this first generation doctor, and my dad kept asking me when I was going to "hang out my shingle."

About this time I wanted to learn more about the business of medicine, those aspects separate from the clinical portions. No doctor seemed to be able to tell me much about that on my rotations as a student or as an intern. So I started to read Business Week and Medical Economics in the library instead of boning up on my anatomy. I found the book, The Tipping Point, by Malcolm Gladwell and Never Eat Alone by Keith Ferrazzi. These books told me stories I had never heard before about things like networking, relationship building, being authentic and personal branding.

I went forward blindly, doing the only thing I knew made others successful. I started networking and talking to people.

THE DOCTOR'S DOCTOR

I went to job fairs, told my running group about my plight, and went to the University guidance counselors. But no one knew what to do with me or what to tell me. I decided that in order to have any credibility in the business world and to learn those skills like marketing, accounting and operations management, I needed to go back to school. So I applied, and was accepted to business school. It was there that I learned how to write a business plan, how to create and maintain a personal development plan, and more about customer relations, quality, networking, etc.

During this time I also looked for opportunities to help other doctors who were unsatisfied with medicine. I saw a story in Physicians Practice, a nationwide journal about non-clinical careers. The next day I e-mailed the editor and began writing articles for them. I also spoke at a conference for doctors – the SEAK Non-clinical conference, about my experience.

Q. Sounds like your passion was growing in your new field.

A. I was breaking through, because I was meeting others who had similar feelings. I was meeting people who admired me. Maybe I wasn't so weak after all! It was starting to become apparent that wasn't the case at all. It was also becoming apparent there was a real need in the world for two things I could do: help doctors find their way and provide a bridge between the business and medical world through some type of consulting. Once I started doing those two things, I found I was working harder than I ever had in medical school, but loving every minute of it. But I also managed to have time to do those things that really mattered to me.

Q. Do you feel like you wasted time in medical school and residency?

A. Looking back, I don't regret going to medical school at all. I realize I just chose a different path. Over the past seven years I have found there are MANY different paths for doctors, but they are not always obvious or articulated. It takes some digging, and even then, they are hard to find.

Q. Do you have any slogans?

A. I now call myself the "Doctor's doctor," because I help physicians find their way in non-traditional roles. This doesn't necessarily mean leaving direct patient care, though it can. It may be as simple as enhancing your life through creating your own personal development plan, finding the right resources, learning some business skills, but not necessarily going back to school. I've seen that every doctor is different. It may take something very simple to empower a burned out, bored, or stressed out doctor, and help open up a whole new world for him or her. I know physicians who have just learned more about information technology and social media, and then obtain a whole new appreciation and excitement for their current practice. I've worked with others who got involved in medical communications which led to them starting their own companies. Others work for the pharmaceutical industry or in the consulting world. There are many different pathways.

It's my job to help doctors find the right pathway for them. I want to use my story, and those of the other doctor's I've helped, to assist others.

Q. Do you have any advice for doctors who want to make the change in their practice?

A. My advice to doctors is this: Have a strategy and employ techniques that work for you. It's not a one-time change or solution. Ask for help and be willing to invest money and time into it. If you've tried once and it didn't work, try again – but in a different way. The definition of insanity is doing the same thing over and over again, and expecting a different result. Reach out to a mentor or someone who understands you, and is willing to spend some time to help you.

And remember there IS hope. Just ask the Doctor's doctor.

THE DOCTOR'S DOCTOR

"I think it's very important that before anyone decides to go from clinical practice to business, they need to do an assessment, an analysis of what it is that they value in their life as a physician. What is important to them?"
Dr. Gabor Oroszlan, Senior Marketing Manager

Dr. Oroszlan, a Native of Hungary is currently a Senior Marketing Manager at Medtronic Diabetes in Los Angeles. He holds an MD from the Semmelweis University and joint MBA/MHA diploma from the University of Minnesota. He has been with Medtronic Diabetes for over 8 years as a Global Business leader and most recently as a product development manager for Insulin Pumps. He is a former member of the Hungarian National Ski Team, and a father of three boys.

Q. When did you graduate from medical school? Did you go directly into clinical practice?
A. I graduated in 1997 in Hungary, Budapest. I did three years as ENT resident, and moved to the US to do research. I did all my licensing tests in the U.S. and in the meantime I began to pursue an MBA. Once I completed that, I was at a crossroads as to which one I wanted to pursue further – a residency here in the U.S. or gravitate towards business.

Q. How did you decide what to do?
A. It was a tough call for me. It might have been even tougher, but I was offered a great opportunity which was so good I couldn't refuse it. It was exactly in line with what I like to do. I chose to join Medtronic as a business unit manager for 13 countries in Eastern Europe. I like to travel and move around a lot. That was one factor I found a little bit discouraging as a physician, going to the same hospital each morning at 7:00

and doing rounds. My life with Medtronic was more what I was looking for, so I did that for about five years, working in countries like Russia, Israel, Poland., Greece – lots of interesting countries. I actually lived in Russia for almost two years. That's why I joined and I don't regret that decision. It really has been the life I was hoping to live.

Q. What was your biggest obstacle to switching to non-clinical?

A. I think the issue as a physician is your experience really doesn't count, right? While you may put in a lot of effort into studying and your practice, you actually risk losing it. The further you go from the field, the more risk you take. I was quite fortunate that Medtronic was a medical device company, so I was still working in the medical field. I had a chance to leverage that on many occasions.

In fact, we have many valuable educators that we work with, so I did a lot of training for them, even though I was a business manager. The business at that time was an entrepreneurial start-up, so I taught patients about our devices. I actually did use my diploma, which was great. Obviously the further I advanced in my career, the less chance I had to stay in touch with patients, but I still do that every once in a while. Right now I am working in the product development process, and the decisions we make on a daily basis will impact hundreds of thousands of patients around the Globe. This is pretty cool.

Q. What was your biggest breakthrough, or piece of advice that you might offer to others?

A. I think it's very important that before anyone decides to go from clinical practice to business, they need to do an assessment, an analysis of what it is that they value in their life as a physician. What is important to them? Why did they choose this profession in the first place? If you don't do that analysis thoroughly, you might get disappointed when you go over to the business side. But if you do analyze it and then conclude, "Yes, a business life is the one for me," then it can be a wise choice. I am actually doing right now what I like the most. I still impact patients on a broader level, but not on a one-on-one basis. There are a lot of patients that I help, by designing the right product for them and that can be fulfilling. You have to be very honest with yourself when you make that decision.

Q. Is there anything else I haven't asked you that you would like to comment on at this time? How does the future look for physicians in your field?

A. I think my field is still a very lucrative area for a physician. Once you are not in practice anymore, you can always emphasize the clinical side of your experience in medical sales or product development. Now that I have a solid business background, I focus on that and consider myself a business person with strong medical background. I am actually trying to keep a balance, which is a delicate thing, but it's fun to do. Yeah, it can be a tough call, but I have found happiness by changing careers. It can be quite rewarding!

Dr. Gabor Oroszlan

"Never mistake knowledge for wisdom. One helps you make a living; the other helps you make a life."

- Sandra Carey

"I am not involved in direct patient care at all. It took awhile to adjust. It was a big culture shock, but now I am really enjoying what I'm doing. I am moving to Spain in August to work for our parent company, Roche."

Dr. Mary Padilla, Cytopathologist

Dr. Padilla earned her M.D. and completed 4 years of residency in Anatomic and Clinical Pathology at the University of Arizona College of Medicine. She completed a Surgical Pathology fellowship and a Cytopathology fellowship at the University of Chicago. Dr. Padilla is board certified in Anatomic and Clinical Pathology and a Fellow of the College of American Pathologists. She practiced Uropathology in a clinical setting prior to making the move to industry. Currently a Principal Pathologist at Ventana Medical Systems, Inc, Mary is a member of the Roche group, in Tucson, Arizona. She recently accepted a new position with Roche Tissue Diagnostics in Europe.

Q. First of all, where did you go to medical school?

A. I went to University of Arizona College of Medicine, graduating in 2001.

Q. What was medical school like for you? Did you find what you were looking for?

A. I went into medicine with an idealistic view of general practice. I thought I wanted to do family practice. I got through my first and second years okay and went to my rotations, but when I got to my family practice rotation, I soon realized this was not anything I would be interested in doing for the rest of my life. So I went into the rural health program during the summer of my third year. I worked out of a family practice office in a rural area, and quickly realized that was

DR. MARY PADILLA

not something I would want to do either. I didn't feel passionate about it. I went into medicine thinking I would do so well and when that didn't work out, I felt a little bit lost. I tried. I rotated through everything and tested them out. I even liked a few things. I really loved surgery the most, but I knew it was not a lifestyle that I wanted. By the end of third year I still wasn't sure, and then I finally did a pathology rotation in Arizona. I really liked it, so I did a second rotation at the University of Michigan and then decided that this was a decent fit for me. I am very visually oriented, so I enjoyed it the most of anything I did.

Q. How much time was there between when you figured out you did not want to be a GP, and when you decided to go into pathology? Was it months or years?

A. I guess it was three years.

Q. So you are now in pathology?

A. Technically yes, but not exactly. I went to a University of Chicago fellowship after my residency in cytopathology. It was one of the most prestigious cytopath fellowships around. I then decided to take a job in Richmond Virginia doing degenerative urinary pathology. That's when I had a light bulb moment. I realized I don't want to do this either!

It took me quite a while to figure that out! I have a very strong personality with pretty good social skills, probably better than the average pathologist. But I found myself going into this office every day and up to the third floor and sitting at my microscope for ten hours straight with no human interaction whatsoever. It got to be a drag for me. Every morning I would wake up and think, "I can't believe I went through all of this schooling to do this!" I really struggled, because I had been given so much training, and I wasn't really qualified to do anything else.

I turned to a career counselor to help me, because I really

PATHOLOGIST

wasn't sure what to do. I think that counselor asked me the right questions. She helped me to clarify for myself what I should do next. She never gave me the answers. It came from me, but she helped clarify things. That was the turning point, when I decided that I wasn't going to do anything I didn't want to do.

About that time, an opportunity came up through somebody that I had known back in Arizona. She told me, "There's this job at a medical company. They need a pathologist. Why don't you come? Maybe you would be interested." There was a cytopath conference in Scottsdale, Arizona, so I decided I would drive down to Tucson to learn more about that job. It turned into a two day interview and a job offer that I had no hesitation in accepting. I have been here for two years now.

Now I work for Ventana Medical Systems and I really love what I do. It is a much better fit for me and it still uses all of my skills from medical school, residency and my fellowship, but in a completely different way. I am not involved in direct patient care at all. It took awhile to adjust. It was a big culture shock, but now I am really enjoying what I'm doing. I am moving to Spain in August to work for our parent company, Roche.

Q. Wow, congratulations on that! Looking back on your transition, what were your biggest obstacles?

A. It was pretty painful when I was going through it. I was miserable. For that one year that I was working, I was really not a happy person. It was a tough decision to make. I think the biggest obstacle was taking the leap and saying, "I am going to change my direction," because once you leave a clinical practice field and not involved in it on a day-to-day basis, there is a perception that you are really losing your skills. If I suddenly changed my mind and decided I wanted to go back to clinical practice, it could be tough for me. I might have to go back and redo a fellowship or something, because now I have been out of it for two years.

But so far that hasn't happened and I am not too worried about it. It was a big decision to actually say, "I am leaving the traditional path of what everyone does in my field. I am going to try out this other thing that is really unheard of." When I joined two years ago there were probably only about a dozen or so pathologists in the world working in that setting, but now that number is growing. It's becoming more of a career opportunity every day, but the biggest leap was to make that conscious choice and stick with it.

Q. So how have your family and friends reacted to your transition from GP to corporate pathologist?

A. My family saw how unhappy I was before. My Dad noticed a couple months after I had been in my new position. He said it was like night and day. I was just so much happier doing what I am doing. My family has always been really supportive, and I talked to some friends from medical school and they were also supportive.

Q. Any advice you can give to others going through a transition? Anything you might like to share?

A. First of all, know that you have options and many marketable skills, even outside of traditional medicine. Know that the traditional route is not for everyone. Second, I would advise getting professional counseling or coaching. I think it is really helpful to bounce ideas off of other people and then listen to their feedback. Sometimes they ask you questions you haven't thought about yet, questions that can help you make your decision. Then, it's a very important thing to be brave and take the leap. Just do it. If it's the right thing to do and what you want to do, then you just have to do it. It all works out somehow, even when it seems like it might not.

PATHOLOGIST

Q. Anything else you would like to talk about before we let you go?

A. I think physicians in particular are trained to be aggressive, working as advocates for their patients. That trait is important as a GP, but in the corporate setting physicians do not work so independently. We need to learn how to be team players, to work in roles where we are not at the top of the totem pole anymore. That takes some getting used to, but I think physicians certainly have the basic skills they need to accomplish that.

DR. MARY PADILLA

"The quality of our lives is determined by the quality of our thinking. The quality of our thinking, in turn, is determined by the quality of our questions, for questions are the engine, the driving force behind thinking. Without questions, we have nothing to think about."

- Dr. Linda Elder and Dr. Richard Paul

19

"Our focus isn't about helping physicians leave medicine or practice...rather, we are interested in exploring what brings them to the point of contemplating leaving, and considering ways that physicians can adjust, augment and enrich their careers and their personal lives so they are more satisfied and more fulfilled."

Dr. Gail Reilly, Transitional Medicine

Gail Reilly, MD is a board certified family physician committed to promoting self-efficacy in medicine by encouraging people to tap into their own power, joy and purpose to allow them to live healthy, fit, active, productive lives. She received her MD from the University of Virginia and completed her family practice residency at the Naval Hospital in Charleston, SC. Dr. Reilly served in the US Navy for 8 years, including a deployment for Operation Desert Storm. She subsequently practiced primary care medicine as a contractor for the US Army for 8 years. In addition to transitioning her medical career, her life includes her husband and 3 children as well as music, gardening and serving in leadership roles in her community.

Q. Why did you go into medicine?

A. Certainly my mother being a nurse had an influence on me. She was always so comfortable with anything that involved health and medicine...it seemed second nature to her. I adopted her comfort and ease about medical matters. She and I still debate about when I decided to become a doctor. She's convinced I wanted to be one from an early age. I remember wanting to be a teacher, and my first recollection of considering medicine was in college! My father was an intellect. He loved contemplating and analyzing and writing, and he was a master wordsmith. His legacy to me is a strong drive for intellectual excellence. When I started selecting college classes, it seemed natural to choose the pre-med classes. I could sign up for either regular science or pre-med science... why not take the higher one? I was naturally drawn towards the coursework, but I wasn't a "hard science" type. I loved my humanities courses. I actually majored in religious studies (one of the best decisions I ever made!) while I continued with my pre-med curriculum.

Eventually, my decision moved from taking pre-med classes to actually considering applying for medical school. In many ways, medicine made so much sense. It was the perfect blend of both the sciences and humanities...it was human science. It was a noble profession, it tapped into my natural altruism, it had prestige, and it appealed to my sense of excellence and my need to achieve very high standards. The die was cast.

Q. So yours was less about growing up wanting to be a doctor, and more about discovering it while you were educating yourself?

A. That's right. I was capable of doing the work, I genuinely liked science and I was drawn towards promoting health. As

I went on, I discovered that I loved the "database" of medical information that I needed to learn. And I believe I am altruistic. It all made sense, so I got on the path and started marching along.

Q. What specialty did you choose?
A. Family practice.

Q. How did that work out for you?
A. One of the most appealing things about medical school for me was the diversity of information we learned. We were exposed to all the specialties and each one held its own wonder and intricacies. I never found myself drawn to one particular specialty, rather, I liked parts of all of them. So when it came time to choose a specialty, family practice seemed the clear answer. It obviated my need to choose. I could maintain clinical diversity in both residency and in my practice.

And perhaps equally as important, I found myself drawn to the type of people that gravitated towards family practice. They seemed the most like me in personality and interests. There was a focus on wholeness and caring for the entire patient, and the concepts of wellness and health promotion were a true priority. There was also a strong sense of "team" in my family practice training...both amongst the physicians practicing as well as between physician and patient. I felt like I fit into this model perfectly.

I don't think I misjudged any of those factors when I made my choice, but I do think (now) that I didn't understand myself very well. As much as I love diversity and variety, I also am highly detail driven and have a strong need to know and understand things very well before I make decisions. I struggled greatly with my inability to have a perfect grasp of the full breadth of family practice. The bandwidth was simply too wide for my comfort zone. It was hard for me to ever feel confident enough (ie. "good enough") to relax into what

DR. GAIL REILLY

I was doing. I was constantly on edge...doubting that I had done enough, read enough or was smart enough to actually practice. It was the classic "imposter syndrome." Someday, someone would actually figure out the truth and expose me for my ineptitude. Fortunately, as with so many physicians, my discomfort and uncertainty actually made me a better doctor because I did go that extra step. I double checked, I spent lots of time making sure I covered everything, and I worried incessantly. I know that I gave really good care...the cost was my own happiness and satisfaction.

Q. Tell me why you did leave medicine?

A. I haven't left medicine...I am adjusting my career path in a direction that is non-clinical. As the GPS says in her pleasant voice..."Recalculating."

It took circumstances to actually encourage my transition. I had been working as a civilian contractor for the military, and the contract ended. It was as simple as that. I didn't make the decision to leave...it just went away! The hard decision was to NOT look for another clinical position in family practice. That one caused me serious angst.

As I look back on it now, there were signs as early as residency that clinical practice might not be the best fit for me. There was a sense of "rightness", dare I say "passion" that was missing. At the time, I chalked it up to being overworked and under-slept. Things did improve somewhat with sleep and experience once I left residency, but there still was a fundamental sense of uneasiness. I didn't settle into clinical practice and enjoy it. Rather, it caused me significant stress and anxiety, much more than I saw in my fellow physicians. And as a result, there was always a sense of dissatisfaction. My patients loved me, I had a reasonable job environment and good life/work balance...yet I found myself filled with foreboding and dread on more days than not. I started to seriously consider whether I should do something different.

TRANSITIONAL MEDICINE

When I found myself no longer employed, it seemed like the perfect time to explore what it would look like to be "happy and fulfilled at work." I had 3 young children at home which validated my decision to not work for awhile. I decided to use the time to explore my options and consider where I wanted to go with my career. I am not leaving medicine or turning away from it. Rather, I am looking towards other ways to use this incredible fund of knowledge that I possess and the skills and experience I developed in clinical practice...ways that allow me to express my other strengths and interests and passions...ways that fill me with joy and a sense of personal purpose.

I've created some wonderful opportunities in the three years since I stopped practicing, and these opportunities have stretched me and helped me better understand myself. Three years ago I couldn't have told you that I love public speaking and teaching, that I love developing and implementing programs and "thinking outside the box" to create new and innovative ways to solve problems and engage change... even that I love writing. It's been a gift to have these opportunities.

Q. Have you been involved in helping other physicians in transition while you are going through your own?

A. It's interesting...once you start talking about transitioning or changing your medical career, other physicians' ears perk up. They are interested. Perhaps they've thought about it or wondered about it, but have been reluctant to speak about it, especially to another physician. Telling my story opens the door to that discussion. Some of my own initial conversations and personal exploration led to an opportunity to address a conference of women physicians and discuss creative ways to use a medical degree. I've also had the privilege of joining two other physicians who are very committed to this unique area of medicine, and together we are working to develop a program that will allow us to carry this discussion to more physicians. Our focus isn't about helping physicians leave medicine or practice...rather, we are interested in exploring what brings them to the point of contemplating leaving, and considering ways that physicians can adjust, augment and enrich their careers and their personal lives so they are more satisfied and more fulfilled...to find ways to be different in medicine or to have a life that is more than medicine.

Q. If you had to give a top three advice list to physicians in transition, what would you say?

A. Perhaps most importantly, "know thyself." Words that come to mind are: self reflection, introspection and discernment. Maybe everyone else has this figured out...I didn't. I had been on "the path"...a very linear path...straight from high school to college/pre-med to medical school to internship to residency to clinical practice with not much in between. That path took a lot of time and a lot of dedication, and, at least in my case, there wasn't much time or encouragement to step outside and be introspective about what I was doing.

There were some "snippets" along the way, as I call them. Moments when my passions and strengths showed through and I saw a bit of my "real self," but they were quickly swallowed up in what needed to be done to stay on the path. In retrospect, I see them clearly as markers and foreshadowing. But it has taken the work of discernment to truly understand who I best am...and it's a work in progress. I'd encourage anyone who is considering transition to spend time thinking, writing, reading, talking, and listening with the intent of self-discovery and self knowledge. It is time well spent.

Secondly, find a mentor...or at least a fellow "transitioner." It's not an easy path to follow, and it's hard to explain to EVERYONE...your parents, your spouse, your friends, your colleagues, the man on the street. Most people can't imagine a doctor that doesn't want to be a "real" doctor...perhaps it ruins their image of Marcus Welby, MD. It's okay for an engineer, or a corporate person, or a teacher or probably even an attorney to want to do something different...but somehow, a physician is sacrosanct, and it is tantamount to heresy to consider being something different. Heck...it's even hard for ME to consider. There's been a lot of pain around this very issue. So, get yourself someone to support you...someone who can hear you out without judgment. It's critical.

Lastly, "try it out." Put your toes (maybe just your big toe!) in the water and see how it feels. I've been fortunate to have this hiatus in my career to do so, but you can do things while you are still practicing. Volunteer at something that lights your fire...add a new facet or side to your practice...experiment doing things differently...whatever it takes. Doing it (even a little bit) is always better than just thinking about it.

Q. Are you approaching transition medicine as a specialty field? You are starting to shape things and give lectures. Do you have any other comments on the evolution and future of transitional medicine?

A. The word transition used in chemistry means a change of state that can involve either a gain or loss of energy; however, matter is conserved and molecular balance is preserved. I hope this definition informs the concept of physician transition. We need to add energy to medical careers and help physicians transition to a new state, yet still preserve the matter...the substrate that makes a physician including their tremendous training and expertise along with their personal gifts...we can't afford to lose that incredible resource. But clearly, there is a need for change. It is different being a physician today...the challenges are different, the expectations are different, the technology is different, medical information is different, even patients are different...than in generations before us. If transition medicine is to be a movement, I hope I can be part of it in a way that helps impart that quanta

DR. GAIL REILLY

of energy ...so that we keep docs in medicine and encourage physician leaders for the next era of health care.

TRANSITIONAL MEDICINE

"Most importantly I learned that it's okay to change directions. It's okay to quit. I think a lot of physicians don't feel able to do that. I think we can begin to feel roped into this."
Dr. Angela Scharnhorst, Health Services Administrator

Angela grew up in Washington State. She obtained a BA from Washington State University and her M.D. at the Medical College of Wisconsin where she did almost 2 years of an emergency medicine residency. Angela has been a member of the Air National Guard for 9 years where she works as a Health Services Administrator. She is currently employed by a large electronic medical records company based in Madison, Wisconsin where she has been working as an implementation project manager.

Q. First of all, what caused you to become a doctor?
A. While growing up I was just fascinated by the human body and science in general. That's where my passion started with medicine. Then I wanted to do something where I could help people, and the combination of the two seemed to be the perfect fit. When I was trying to make the decision to go to medical school, I was actually trying to decide between being a mom or a doctor. At that time I didn't have a boyfriend, so I decided that medicine would be the right path for me.

Q. How did you pick emergency medicine?
A. I liked the variety of it. I wanted to be the first person to lay my hands on a person and make a diagnosis. I liked the idea of never turning anybody away and accepting everyone regardless of their insurance status.

Q. Did you enjoy being an ER doc?
A. I got almost through my second year of residency before I realized it was not for me. I probably realized first during my

intern year, but I just wasn't ready to admit it yet. When I start something, I feel like I have to finish it.

Q. What was missing?

A. I don't think I had the personality for it. I have thought about that a lot. I've tried to figure out what it was exactly. I think I got too wrapped up in my patients and their families and I took it all home with me. I was not good at separating myself, and that caused a lot of stress in my personal life.

It was a very hard decision. I took two leaves of absences and tried to go back, but it just never worked out. I finally had to say, "Enough is enough."

Q. So what was next for you?

A. I became pretty disillusioned. I had no idea what I wanted to do with my life, and I didn't have the option of doing nothing because of my student loans, so I decided to take some time off. I was fortunate to have a husband with a good job during this time, while I was trying to figure out what to do next with myself. He was very supportive and he paid the bills while I was doing my soul searching.

I began putting myself out there, doing internet research, networking with people and just trying to figure out what I felt passionate about. When I was in my emergency medicine residency, we implemented an electronic record system and I was a part of the implementation team. I really enjoyed that kind of work. It was something I was interested in and could get excited about. I enjoyed my shifts when I worked on that. So, it just happened that when I was searching for a job, I threw out on Facebook a random post – "Does anybody know of any jobs?" Someone responded with, "There's an electronic medical company that is always hiring." So I applied and got hired.

HEALTH SERVICES ADMIN / PROJECT MANAGER

It's been a rough year for sure. So that was really exciting for me. In the interim though, I am in the Air Force and International Guard, so I was on active duty for a couple months. I went through training to be an Air Force health care administrator. I do that on the side.

Q. Is it tough being in the military?
A. Yes, but it doesn't seem too bad. I haven't been deployed. What I have been doing so far has not been that difficult. I have just been doing a lot of paperwork and helping out with the meetings and such at the clinic.

Q. Do you see more of a future in IT for yourself?
A. Yes I do. It's hard for me to say, but from what I have seen so far, I think this may be a good path for me.

Q. What kind of position do you see yourself in?
A. I think more of a corporate position. My actual position now is implementation consultant.

Q. That's a very different culture. Is it taking time to get used to?
A. It's kind of hard to say right now, but from a military standpoint I can say that this particular career path has been very easy to adjust to. I like the administrative role so far.

Q. So you went from medical school to a very different field. What did you learn through this process that you could share with others?
A. Most importantly I learned that it's okay to change directions. It's okay to quit. I think a lot of physicians don't feel able to do that. I think we can begin to feel roped into this. One of the women I went to medical school with said it felt kind of like a gang. You may get started in it, and then you just can't get out! But if you are not happy, and I see so many bitter physicians who feel trapped, you need to know when

enough is enough and admit that maybe this isn't what you were meant to do. That was the hardest thing for me to do. It's still hard for me, and I still have thoughts of going back, just so I can finish.

Q. That might go away when you see how much better you will sleep and how well rested you feel. Emergency medicine is great, but it will definitely burn your nerve endings in time.

A. Yes. I burned out at a very rapid rate. Usually it takes a few years, so I guess looking back, I was lucky to figure it out sooner rather than later. But it would have been nice to get my medical school loans paid off first though.

Q. Were there any guiding slogans that kept you on target getting through those tough times?

A. I like, "Easy does it," and "It is what it is." I've got a bunch of them – "Live and let live." I think my favorite one has been, "It is what it is." Any time I get upset or have a tough time, I just say that to myself.

21

"I've learned that it is helpful to have an attitude of being authentically committed to the welfare, health and wellbeing of others first. That circles back around."

Dr. Mark Schnitzer, International Trainer

Dr. Schnitzer is a Johns Hopkins-trained, board certified neurosurgeon. After successfully creating a practice in Southern California, he realized that many colleagues and other professionals were finding it harder to get ahead with corporate downsizing, lack of job security, falling reimbursement, and the higher cost of living. In 2005 Dr. Schnitzer began teaching cash flow classes to entrepreneurial professionals, helping them set up their own businesses, so they could start taking care of themselves and their families once again. Dr. Schnitzer has become an internationally-known leader and trainer in professional network marketing. Dr. Schnitzer invites inquiries from the curious and skeptical as well as the entrepreneurial and self-motivated.

Q. Just briefly, what happened after medical school? What specialty did you chose?

A. After medical school I went to the Johns Hopkins Hospital in neurosurgery. Simultaneously with that, towards the end I did a neuroscience critical care fellowship.

DR. MARK SCHNITZER

At the end, when I was chief resident, I had an offer to be the co-head of the intensive care unit at Duke or I could go into private practice in California.

The thought went through my head. It takes three things to be a good ivory tower doctor, the ability to be a good family person, the ability to do research, and the ability to take care of your patients. I could do any two of them, but not all three of them. So, I chose to be a private practice doctor because I wanted to take care of patients and have a family. I gave up on the ivory tower gig early on and became a private practice doctor in California.

Q. How did that go for you? Was it satisfying?

A. Not really. I was recruited to join a big medical group, but I would have been the only neurosurgeon. My intention was to meet the local neurosurgeon and find out if we could arrange cross-cover before I accepted the job. Low and behold, the local neurosurgeon was a big shot in the American Association of Neurological Surgeons. After a couple hours, they offered to hire me away. They wanted to hire me to work with him. The arrangement was that I would work for them for a year as an employee and at the end of the year I would be a partner, so there would be no buy-ins or anything like that.

What happened, to my great shock and surprise, they ripped me off. They really took advantage of me. After a year and a half I said, "Hey look, it's been over a year. It's time to get this corrected." They said, "Okay, here is your buy-in," but it was not what we had agreed to from the beginning. I said,

> "...you see further when you stand on the shoulders of giants."

"Hey you guys, it's been fun. How about we continue to cross-cover each other, but I'm going to go set up my own shop."

INTERNATIONAL TRAINER

It was remarkable. I was really surprised. Overnight I had to set up my own shop. I got a Kelly girl for a secretary and I had a timeshare office. I thought my employee was the greatest thing since sliced bread. Her desk was immaculate. She was attractive and smiling and everyone loved her. Then, after she left, I found a big box of faxes, bills and checks unopened. It was amazing!

I survived that and have done well. I had no mentor. I think that is the biggest deficiency, not having a proper mentor. I don't remember who said it but, you see further when you stand on the shoulders of giants. I wish I had had a mentor early on. I also recognize that it is not too late. I am 50 years old. I am willing to sit at the knee of a master, because I learn quickly and I'd love to be a mentor to others.

Q. Are you currently in private practice or are you doing something different at this time?

A. I am in my practice while endeavoring to transition into something else.

Q. So you are actually in transition? Do you have a mentor? Have you found those websites helpful to you personally?

A. I have been a member of the American College of Physician Executives for about fifteen years, and I've taken their classes. I guess early on my intention was to transition out of the clinical venue by the time I was forty. That was ten years ago. I need to do this. I've been involved in hospital government, but not in a paid administrative way.

Q. What have you learned so far in your transition?

A. I've learned that it is helpful to have an attitude of being authentically committed to the welfare, health and wellbeing of others first. That circles back around. If you give away 90% of your content, people will pay you for the other 10%. I'm certain of this truth. This attitude has given me access to very talented and successful people who are happy to talk

DR. MARK SCHNITZER

to me, because I'm not asking them for anything. In fact, I am offering them something. My intention is to become a valuable resource so that they will choose to offer me mentoring, hire me or partner with me. Ultimately I'd rather be the owner than the employee. You have to take small steps, but I'm not adverse to that. I don't know what will come from participating with you. Something good will happen, because if you put out good stuff, good stuff comes back.

Q. I think someone else said just get your foot in the door. Work for free if you have to and the money will come later. Are you are still trying to find an executive positions?

A. I have no doubt about my ability to quickly grow into any kind of position, if they are willing to train and mentor me. I also have an engineering background. I have a MS degree in electrical engineering. That essentially makes me an interface professional, someone who is conversant in both geek and doctor. I'm looking forward to a meeting with a couple of people who are part of an organization that is comprised of doctors, engineers and venture capitalists, people who develop products that are ultimately brought to market. I think it is important to do things that you can have fun doing. Because then, you don't mind the hours and it's really not so much work.

Q. What do you see in your future? What will you be doing in ten years?

A. In ten years I intend to own a very large international company that someone wants to buy from me. I don't know what it will look like. It doesn't have to be in medicine. It could be and I would be happy with that, but I know I have certain skill sets and I'm willing to work. There are certain aspects of being a businessman I'm not familiar with. One way to acquire them would be to partner with people who already know business.

I have been on the short end of the stick before with people whom I trusted but they took advantage of me. I don't consider failure a bad thing, but I do consider mediocrity to be a bad thing. Failure is just the other side of the success coin. I'm willing to fall as long as I keep getting back up. Eventually I will encounter people who are looking for the same things that I am looking for and are trustworthy. I want to make a contribution, earn a lot of money, and have an excellent exit strategy.

DR. MARK SCHNITZER

"If you want to move people, it has to be toward a vision that's positive for them, that taps important values, that gets them something they desire..."

- Martin Luther King, Jr.

"I was a little slow getting out of the gate. I made the decision but, looking back, I should have prepared for that decision way in advance. I did not anticipate that this transition would take as long as it has. It's really been a learning process."

Dr. Andrew Schwartz, Holistic Clinician

Andrew M. Schwartz, M.S., M.D. is a graduate of City University of New York and Georgetown University School of Medicine. A board certified cardiothoracic surgeon in clinical practice for 21 years, his focus in heath care today is centered around patient safety and quality of care. Dr. Schwartz serves as a medical consultant in multiple venues that include Cardiac Wellness and early detection screening for lung cancer. "I have become a holistic clinician who seeks to bridge the connection between the body and mind with spirituality.

Q. Why did you decide to become a physician?

A. In 1967, at age 13, Dr. Christian Barnard performed the first heart transplant. That really piqued my interest in medicine. Through the ensuing years I found myself being steadily interested in medicine and in the heart, but I was not certain what my future might entail. Along the way I got involved with the American Heart Association and that led to a relationship with a cardiologist in my community. That relationship created numerous opportunities to work in a local hospital. One summer, I spent two and a half months in the Department of Cardiology. During that summer, I had the opportunity to watch heart surgery and that really did it for me. That set the foundation for what would lead me to become a practicing cardiothoracic surgeon.

Along the way I remember taking the long part of the stethoscope that goes to the diaphragm, and attaching it to the narrow end of a metal funnel that I had taken from my mother's kitchen. On the wide open end or the wide mouth of the funnel I attached a microphone that was attached to a tape recorder. Then I used window caulking to seal where the microphone attached to the funnel and then I was able to record human heart sounds. I created the ability to perform echocardiograms. That was kind of neat.

Q. It sounds like you picked your specialty before you picked your medical school?

A. Absolutely, yes. But I was the average B student, nothing to write home about...

Q. You chose your specialty practice and you've been practicing for how many years now?

A. Twenty-one years.

Q. Have you achieved what you set out to in your profession as a cardiothoracic surgeon?

A. Absolutely. I have had the opportunity to do what I dreamed of and then some. The most enjoyable part of practicing cardiothoracic surgery was not in the operating room, but the interactions I was able to have with patients and their loved ones. I left clinical practice as of March 2009. I'm very comfortable with that decision, but I do miss my interactions with patients and their families. Through clinical practice, I had the opportunity to be very involved in the life of the hospital, medical staff and with leadership, patient safety, quality, etc. Those are some of the interests I found that continued to grow stronger as my interest in clinical practice waned. These experiences were a great source of enjoyment, satisfaction and fulfillment, and served in part as an impetus to get involved in hospital leadership and to search for a CMO or VPMA position.

Q. So it sounds like there was a clear path for you? A door just opened up and you had all the right reasons to pursue it?

A. Unlike my decision to go into cardiothoracic surgery, which developed as an ever-growing desire, this element was something I did not have and nor was I seeking. I didn't start out saying, "I really want to do this. I will see what I need to do to be involved in physician leadership". It started out as involvement on different committees that dealt with patient safety, quality of care and peer review, which I found increasingly fulfilling. As time went on I became more involved by choice. Then members of the Hospital and Medical Staff leadership started to approach me for my opinions and perspectives on different projects and to expand my involvement in committee work and physician leadership.

Q. So you made the decision in 2009. What are you doing now? Are you looking for a job at this time?

A. I was a little slow getting out of the gate. I made the decision to transition from clinical practice to a physician leadership position 4-5 years earlier, but, looking back, I should have better prepared myself for that decision, especially an exit strategy, way in advance. I did not anticipate that this transition would take as long as it has. It's really has been a learning process.

I interviewed with a recruiter two weeks ago and explained, "You know, this is really new territory for me." I've never

DR. ANDREW SCHWARTZ

175

really interviewed for a position in this way. When I interviewed for a job in cardiac surgery, basically it was a matter of assessing my performance in school and during surgical training. I obviously had recommendations from people from my fellowship and general surgery training programs, but, this current process is very different. The number of cardiothoracic surgeons that were needed when I finished my fellowship, which has significantly increased today, was such that I knew I would get a job, it was just a matter of where.

This is really different. It's been a learning process. A recruiter recommended that I should have had a lot more interviews than I have had so far. She said one of my problems was that I using a CV rather than a résumé, which includes more of an explanation of my responsibilities, my goals, my successes, etc. I really needed to be educated on how to search for a job. So, everything is new. The interviewing process continues to be in evolution for me. I interviewed for a CMO position in Florida in March. The CEO addressed my candidacy and what was lacking in my application. He cited two things: the interviewers had trouble appreciating why I wanted to transition from a practicing cardiothoracic surgeon to a CMO or VPMA of a hospital and they found me to be a little long-winded in my responses. Sometimes I do wander away from the questions and I don't get to the main issue. I acknowledge this, because there are times when I wonder, "Did I answer that question?"

I recently got a call from a company here in Kansas, about fifteen minutes away. They offered me a part-time job as a medical consultant. Somehow they found me. I was up front with the company and informed them that my true love is being in a hospital and serving in a position such as a VPMA or CMO.

Q. What have been your toughest obstacles while in transition? How have your family and friends reacted to this transformation from a doctor to executive?

A. My wife had some trouble accepting the fact that I really wanted to make this transition. She saw me as an individual who really loved what I was doing for so many years. I'm a very good technical surgeon and I'm an excellent physician. "We" are now one year into this process, and she now accepts it. She has always been supportive of my career decisions.

My daughter is going into her senior year of high school this August, and my son will be in 10th grade. My daughter desires to be able to finish out her last year of high school in Kansas. So, we decided early on that the most likely scenario is that I will move first and the family will follow. Is that optimal? No, but we have discussed this multiple times, and they understand the potential for this happening. They have been very supportive.

A number of my close friends who are physicians have difficulty understanding my decision to leave cardiac surgery for a "less prestigious" job as a physician executive and my willingness to take a large salary cut. That's not my take. I just want to go to a job each morning that I really enjoy and where I feel I can have a positive impact. I would like the opportunity to impact an entire hospital and the surrounding community, physicians, staff, patients, and beyond. I see that as a wonderful opportunity.

With all the bumps in the road, it sometimes feels depressing, especially the rejections. I will go on an interview and when I get home my wife will ask, "How did it go?" and I will say, "I think it went pretty well." Then I'll find out I didn't get the job. I've had some feedback, but most people are reluctant to say anything. Many places want someone who has prior experience or want someone who has practiced in

DR. ANDREW SCHWARTZ

health care environment where there is a physician executive leader.

Q. Do you have any advice for other physicians contemplating change?

A. First, you have to establish what it is you want to do. If you leave clinical practice saying, "I want something else," and you have no clear decision about what you want to explore next, that can be problematic unless you are fiscally well positioned and you have the luxury of time. I knew what I wanted to do, but I should have been working on my résumé and applications ahead of time. I should have started the process before I actually left clinical practice. I would encourage doctors who are seeking to make this type of transition, to prepare them well before they leave clinical practice.

Second, remember that a transition is not a "solo act" and that your loved ones are part of this process. Your decisions don't only affect you!

Third, I think it is important to follow your heart and do something that is going to bring you a lot of satisfaction. You and I have both experienced physicians who just can't stand practicing medicine anymore. The senior surgeon in our group retired just short of 50 years of age. He was fortunate. He practiced in the "heyday" of reimbursement for cardiac surgery. He really hated what he was doing. He left practice and he is doing a lot of satisfying things, but, nothing related to health care. He is doing things that bring him a lot of enjoyment. He is very active in young adult athletic programs. He has taken up wood carving. That might sound funny, but he is very happy with what he is doing now.

It's tough when you have grown accustomed to a certain lifestyle and then you have to make decisions that might compromise that. That can be scary. For me, my greatest concern is to enjoy what I am doing in an environment that allows me to continue to contribute to health care and the happiness of my family.

Dr. Andrew Schwartz

"Before you become unstoppable for others, you must become unstoppable for yourself."

- Unknown

"I realized I wanted to start a wellness program. I had no idea where to begin, but I started anyway. That's one of my key things. If you have a passion or a dream, just start in that direction. Put your sail up and start sailing."
Dr. Kelly Sennholz, Founder, Chief Medical Officer

Kelly Z. Sennholz MD is Founder and Chief Medical Officer of Symtrimics, a "Physician Directed Wellness" program. She has assisted thousands to obtain the excellent health they have always desired. Working with Symtrimics, she has also accomplished her dream of helping other doctors regain control of their patient's health and regain control of their own practice. By establishing a "Practice Within a Practice," doctors are able to dramatically improve their patient's health and free themselves from relying 100% upon outside reimbursements for their practice income. This provides them with not only increased time and financial freedom, but most importantly, the freedom to spend quality time with each of their patients.

Q. Where did you go to medical school?

A. I grew up in Wisconsin and went to medical school in Oklahoma. Soon after graduation, I moved to North Carolina where I practiced most of my active medical career.

Unlike many of my fellow students, I already had a family and a life before entering school, which was a very different experience.

Q. Why did you want to become a physician?

A. Well, I was working as a nurse and I felt passionate about helping people. I realized that since I was six years old, I just loved helping people see the possibilities in their lives. I enjoyed helping them to smile or just have a better day. That's what makes me tick.

Q. How did you choose your specialty practice after med school?

A. I completed an internship in Pediatrics and Internal Medicine and finished a residency in Internal Medicine. As a single mother, I realized that the typical life of a physician wasn't going to fit very well with my parenting duties. I began working in emergency medicine at the invitation of an esteemed group in our hospital. I just fell in love with it, and ended up working in that field my entire medical career.

Q. So when did you decide it was time to switch to a different passion?

A. During my career I did just about everything that anybody would find interesting in medicine. I mean I worked in neonatal, pediatrics, internal medicine, emergency medicine, and I worked as a hospitalist. I became president of my local medical society and was on their board for seven years. I was on the state board of emergency physicians. I independently created legislation in two different states. I created financing for a clinic for the working poor for 5 years. I have done everything you can find interesting in medicine. I kept waiting for the punch line, I guess you would say. I kept think-ing that if I work hard and work my way up the ladder, I am going to find that sweet spot where I can really make a dif-ference. What I found instead was that medicine had been so infiltrated with the pharmaceutical paradigm that we had gone way off track in our mission to keep people healthy. I remember leaving many of those medical meetings thinking, "What did we just accomplish?" And often, the answer was absolutely nothing.

Then a couple of things happened. About six years ago now, I was working the night shift with another physician who had been an ER doctor forever. He's a really great doctor, and it's 3:00 a.m., and there's a drunk guy spitting on him. This doc is 65 years old with bad knees and I looked at him and thought, "This is so not me! I am not going to be 65 years old at 3:00 in the morning having a drunken guy spit on me." So I started to realize that I needed to find something else to do, something that would fulfill my heart and my spirit.

Then another thing happened. I ended up getting a thing called transverse myelitis. I became paralyzed on the left side of my body for 6 months. At that time, I had already be-gun my path out of clinical medicine by setting up a medical spa. Many doctors have chosen that as a way out and I was no different. Except, I had fortunately decided to include a wellness program within the spa.

With my illness, I was able to experience the medical sys-tem from the viewpoint of a patient and to say I was unim-pressed is to greatly underestimate my experience. If I had not been a physician with the know how to fight back and get what I wanted, I probably could be in a wheel chair with bowel and bladder insufficiency right now. Just before this all happened, I remember a patient coming up to me one night in the ER. It was crazy busy, but I was having a good night. This patient said, "Dr. Sennholz, what kind of vitamins do you take?" I just looked at her and said, "I don't know – Centrum." She looked at me with this absolutely disgusted look as if to say "You don't know anything, do you?"

I realized I didn't know anything about health, diet, exercise or supplements. In fact I didn't know anything about physical therapy, occupational therapy or most of the other therapies my patients were getting referred to. I didn't know if their therapies worked for them. I didn't know if they were getting any benefit. I started to ask more questions. I heard that patients were coming back again and again to get steroid shots for their knee arthritis, but nobody was doing anything at all to make sure that they exercised or lost some weight, or started taking glucosamine. Nobody was doing anything to prevent their problems, they were just giving them more pain medications.

I started to become frustrated with my own profession. Those three experiences came at me all at once. I knew for certain that I wanted to get out of ER medicine. I got an illness and experienced the medical profession from the inside, and I began to realize that what we were doing was what others were accusing us of, putting a patch on things and not fixing anything.

That grew into my medical spa. I realized I wanted to start a wellness program. I had no idea where to begin, but I started anyway. That's one of my key things. If you have a passion or a dream, just start in that direction. Put your sail up and start sailing. Did I make mistakes along the way? Yes, of course. Did I learn things as I went along? Yes, but by starting that program I began to work with patients. I would ask other doctors, "Dr. Smith, in your practice, how many patients have you assisted to lose 60 to 100 pounds, get off diabetic medications, get off hypertensive medications, etc.?" And every doctor answered they had only assisted 0 to 1 patients to accomplish these goals in their whole career. By this time, I was doing this on a regular basis with my patients and understood there was a systematic way to accomplish this for which the physician could actually be paid for their time. This was the realization that I could not only help patients to become healthy, but I could also give other doctors the tools they need to help their patients become healthy, too.

Q. So you had your passion there, right in front of your face in your own clinic?

A. Right in front of my face. I opened up my heart and it walked right in the door. I recently read the books Blink and Outliers by Malcolm Gladwell. These books are really good. Outliers is about the circumstances that cause you to get where you are. Traits like intelligence and good personality are a dime a dozen, but opportunity is what happened to me. I fell into this. It was always an interest, but I fell into this at just the right time and at the right place. The thing Gladwell talks about in his book is the fact that people who are successful, consistently first have 10,000 hours of work and experience under their belt before they become an overnight sensation. For example, the Beatles may have seemed like an overnight sensation, but they had played seven days a week in clubs for years before success arrived. They had 10,000 hours under their belt. People like Bill Gates had many opportunities come his way, but not before he had 10,000 hours of coding under his belt. And I believe at this point in time I have 10,000 hours under my belt.

Q. It sounds like you are pretty much a self-starter here. Did you require any outside help – mentoring, coaching, career advice, anything of that nature?

A. Absolutely! Along my entire career, I have been blessed with the appearance of many talented and giving people who have helped me along. My very first mentor was named one of the top fifty people of the century during the millennium celebrations! It's just like in the book Outliers. I just hap-

DR. KELLY SENNHOLZ

pened to be in the right place at the right time. Her name was Wilma Mankiller. She was the first woman chief of the Cherokee nation, and she was a force to be reckoned with. Such a wonderful woman! I got to work with her even before I was out of medical school.

I felt it was extremely important to find good mentors, and I looked for them in the business field. One of my 'mentors' was actually a class that I took, called The Legacy Center (thelegacycenter.com). That class helped me pair down to the very core of what makes me tick and what makes me passionate. It taught me how to create that in my life and taught me that there were no limits to my life.

Q. Did that class take several weeks?
A. The class is offered in 3 parts. The first part is 5 days. The second important part is 5 days. Then, I received daily coaching for 3 months, along with one weekend a month away at class. It is a life leadership class which taught me much about how to create my life, rather than living a life of reaction. It was a powerful experience which has changed the way I see the world and the way I show up for people.

Q. Do you do any mentoring or coaching?
A. You know, I love mentoring people. Just like a lot of people who become physicians, I really do enjoy helping people and making a difference for them in their lives. It's my passion. I am open to mentoring when I see someone really wants to change and needs a little push in the right direction.

Regarding our program, I love our doctors. I love helping them escape the bonds of the health insurance system. I love helping them regain their joy in medicine and their joy in taking care of people again. I love helping them find a way to utilize their skills and make money at it while enjoying their practice again.

FOUNDER / CHIEF MEDICAL OFFICER

186

Q. While going through your transition, what was your biggest obstacle to overcome?

A. Many doctors come to me for advice on how to transition out of medicine. But I have found that doctors as a group have very analytical personalities. What happens is that they may have a dream or idea, but when they start down the road, they ask far too many questions which can paralyze them from taking action. It is one thing to know a subject well enough to act but quite another to spend so much time ruminating that the opportunity just passes by you.

Sometimes with doctors the best thing is to just to take a leap of faith, or push them off the cliff, with the understanding that they need to put some money away for the journey before they leap. They need to understand that failure of any dream is a possibility. We all experience failure along the way, and that's okay. Be humble and just get out there and make it happen.

One thing that really helped me was taking that class. If I hadn't, there were so many points where I might have second guessed myself. Perhaps I would have questioned what I was doing, been less clear about my mission, and because of that I probably could have failed at any one of many points along the way. Because I was very clear about what I wanted to create, those obstacles never held me down.

Q. What about prevention and wellness? Is that a growing field? Are physicians gravitating towards that area of medicine?

A. Massively. One of the mistakes I see physicians making repeatedly is what I call the "Lone Ranger Syndrome." When they decide to go into wellness, they feel they need to create their own program. So they stop everything, and spend 2,000 hours putting a program together, when there are a multitude of resources out there to choose from. They hire

DR. KELLY SENNHOLZ

a nutritionist, which is a cost center, not a profit center. They spend a tremendous amount of time and effort trying to reinvent the wheel. They fail because they get exhausted and they run out of money. Being able to utilize some turn-key options that are already out there is important.

> "It is one thing to know a subject well enough to act but quite another to spend so much time ruminating that the opportunity just passes by you."

Before they know about Symtrimics, they always want to private label everything, and become a 'guru'. That is the lone ranger thing. They think they have to invent a new concept or product, which is simply not true. What they do have to do is make a choice and work it to the best of their abilities. Private labeling, overall, does not work. Often, the results are high costs, low results and a garage full of materials. I know lots of people that private-labeled skin care products or some other type of product, and I have yet to see one of them make a big financial gain on them. I'm sure there are exceptions, but in my experience, they are rare exceptions. So my best advice would be, stop thinking that you have to re-invent the wheel! We love to assist them to learn the subject, outsource all the work and development and find the part of it that really resonates with them and build upon that. Now, that is a path that can lead to success.

Q. **Is there anything on the horizon for the future of wellness medicine? Any trends we should know about?**
A. This is certainly an exciting field right now. I will tell you this: Look at the NIH statistics for obesity in our country. The obesity rate was below 10% in the majority of states only twenty years ago, and they are close to 30% in most states now. This is devastating, financially, physically, and emotionally. Busi-

ness journals are writing frequently about how, if we don't get a handle on it, diabetes alone will bankrupt our nation in a short period of time.

But when the government decides to fix this, they go to corporations, not doctors. They go to corporations for a couple of reasons: one is that physicians tend to have little understanding of the business world. They don't understand how things work so they end up being very hard to work with. As a group, they are not educated in the way business works, so they can often make very basic business errors that create impatience in those who are more skilled in these fields. Secondly, they are behind the curve, big time, when it comes to a deep understanding of how to change the health of patients and communities. We weren't taught this in medical school or residency. As a group, physicians have no basis from which to begin. So going to corporations seems easier.

The fact is physicians need to take back the practice of wellness medicine. Physicians deal with illness on a daily basis. We see the results of obesity. We see diabetes. We talk to people. We know how to read and interpret studies. These are our patients, and so we are the ones who should step up and lead this fight. We need to give physicians a platform, give them a voice and help them understand how to project that voice through the internet, through television, radio – and become the voice of health and wellness.

I am passionate about that, too. Physicians need to take back wellness to create healthier patients, healthier communities and a healthier nation. This is really at the core of what being a doctor is, and somewhere around the pharmaceutically financed pizza in anatomy class we lost sight of it. Symtrimics is designed to help doctors reestablish control over their patient's health and their medical practice's health.

Dr. Kelly Sennholz

Q. Right, and having a corporation with multiple centers, you have a different level of quality to offer to your patients?

A. We are able to put nearly a $120,000 of Fortune 500 style marketing into each of our practices for free, because of the scalability of our business. Our whole job is to make doctors successful. We teach, support, market and maintain the background for each physician's success. Our goal is to make each doctor the "Dr Oz" of their community. We want them to be the physician that television, radio and newspapers think of when they need a quote for wellness or medicine. We want the community to see them as doctors who really care about the health of their patients and are not there to just write prescriptions. That is the support we give our doctors.

Q. Fantastic – where do I sign up?

A. You would have to talk to one of my sales people. We focus on OB GYN and Plastics, but any practice with a healthy number of patients and a motivated physician is a great prospect for this opportunity. There are many ways to approach this and to be honest, each practice has individualized needs and desires that make it very unique. I love that part. This can be quite lucrative. I mean, by the time I did this for six months I was making more money residually than I made as a physician. My goals have obviously expanded, but my goal for every single physician is to do the same thing, to set them up so that they have enough residual income coming in from this program, that they can walk away from their practice- -if they want to. Creating that power within your practice sure changes one's attitude. When you have the freedom to walk away, then medicine can become a joy again.

Q. What sort of training programs do you have for physicians transitioning into wellness?

A. Symtrimics goes in for a training period before the launch occurs. We have educational programs for staff and for physicians. We even have individual educational websites for each. We physically go to their office and evaluate it. We have a massive amount of marketing that we employ during this period, to advertise for the launch. We do it within about three weeks and then we launch. Sometimes I will fly into the city and do a patient centered speaking engagement for the launch. Other times they just want to do the launch privately with the assistance of our sales people. So it varies and it's tailored to the practice.

We tend to focus on OB-GYN because every woman influences twenty people in her life, health-wise. Our goal is not simply to improve a doctor's practice, but we are dead serious about the fact that when we go into a community, we rock the health of the entire community. I just reviewed the physical findings from one of our first cities and the average weight loss was something like 50 pounds over 8 weeks. These patients lost this weight healthfully and without pain or hunger. The average cholesterol drop was 30. We had some patients drop four to five hundred points off their triglycerides. Average glucose drop was 30. These are profound numbers that will be maintained over time. This is not a diet, it is a physician directed, lifelong, comfortable health program. Once our doctors begin to see they can make these radical changes with their patients by merely starting them on the program, now that's when it gets exciting.

DR. KELLY SENNHOLZ

"The greatest danger for most of us is not that our aim is too high and we miss it, but that it is too low and we reach it."

- Michelangelo

"Once I was open to change and had a vision for it, the universe responded and helped me find my way to where I am now."

Dr. Rebecca Winokur, Senior Clinical Content Editor

Dr. Winokur is currently a Senior Clinical Content Editor and Clinical Lead for Allscripts, an electronic health record company. She received a BA from Colby College, an MA from Boston University School of Medicine and an MD from the University of Vermont School of Medicine. She is also an Assistant Professor for the Department of Family Medicine at Fletcher Allen Health Care. Rebecca was formerly a primary care sports medicine physician at Associates in Orthopedic Surgery. She has been the recipient of both teacher appreciation and the AAFP Pfizer Foundation teacher of the year. In her spare time, she raises money and awareness for the health care crisis in Ethiopia.

Q. Where did you go to medical school?
A. I went to the University of Vermont College of Medicine in Burlington, VT.

Q. When did you graduate?
A. In 2000.

DR. REBECCA WINOKUR

Q. Did you go into a specialty after that?

A. I did. I completed a residency in Family Medicine in Burlington, VT and immediately from there completed a fellowship in Primary Care Sports Medicine in Portland, ME.

Q. So you were on your way to becoming a practicing physician?

A. I was and I thought that sports medicine was the way to go. I found a nice job after my sports fellowship, in an orthopedic practice. I saw all of the non-surgical patients, mostly injured athletes. The problem was that after all of that training, I did not love what I was doing and I was in the best clinical setting I could have imagined.

Q. Was it the whole patient care picture or was there anything specific for you?

A. The biggest issue was not being able to take care of people the way that I wanted to. I only dealt with one part of their problem, the physiologic part. I never got to work with a team of health care professionals who could help with things like the context of their problem, the psycho-social aspects that affect healing and recovery as much as anything else. There was no collaborative team approach. I found that hard to accept.

I just felt like I couldn't practice medicine like that. Add to that, the notion that my work was never done. I didn't have tangible results or completed projects. If a patient got better, I didn't see them again. And those who did not get better expected me to work miracles. It just did not suit me.

Q. You finally had to leave medicine after these driving forces. So, what happened next?

A. I admitted to myself that I needed to make a change but it took a few years before I could say it aloud. It was the notion that I couldn't keep going like this for 30 years. It was not happiness. I needed to take action. First, I found out about a conference lead by SEAK, for other physicians like me. Then I started poking around on line. I found lots of resources and realized that there were many others sharing this sentiment and desire to shift their focus from clinical medicine to something more suitable.

Q. Did you follow the process that SEAK had laid out?

A. I attended the 2007 conference. It was a great starting place. After the conference, I read the handouts and worked through the workbook assignments. I then connected with some of their references regarding people to help with career coaching and resume building. I found a fantastic career coach, Philippa Kennealy. She worked with me for several months.

Q. What was that experience like for you?

A. Working with my career coach was amazing. And it was really fun. She helped me sort out what I wanted to do and how to get organized and move towards what I wanted. She taught me how to network and how to ask for help. Once I could articulate what it was that I wanted, it became pretty easy and natural to ask people for help. I set about looking for work that fit my values, including continuing to contribute to the betterment of how we deliver health care.

Maybe it was serendipity, or maybe it was my openness to it and readiness for it, but my new non-clinical job fell into my lap. I had done several informational interviews, and soon found my current job. When I met my future manager and the company's Chief Medical Officer, I knew that this was the job for me. It was a relief and a thrill when I was offered the job.

I've been at it for awhile now and still find it fun and satisfying. I work on a team, we collaborate and leverage each other's strengths. I contribute regularly to our company's goal of improving health care delivery. I use my medical knowledge

DR. REBECCA WINOKUR

and clinic experience every day. The potential for me in this company is huge and it's exciting to challenge myself and participate in health information technology development as the need is huge and the potential is great. I don't have a single regret.

Q. Describe what is different about your job now.

A. The most notable difference is that I am now part of a team of people who all work towards the same goal. We collaborate, trouble shoot and help each other to succeed. I don't carry the burden of any one problem by myself anymore. I'm part of a team that is trying to solve things together. If I hit a wall, there is someone there who can help me. It's much more satisfying to me in this way. I also feel like I'm having a bigger impact on health care on a more global level from the health information technology perspective.

Q. You are still involved in clinical medicine, but just in a different environment and structure?

A. Yes, I'm involved in clinical medicine in two ways. I still practice one night a week to maintain my clinical skills. This is in an urgent care setting affiliated with our local hospital. In my job at Allscripts, I build clinical content for one of our EHR's. In our content development cycles, I work with physician clients to optimize the content. Each specialty has different needs and I translate those needs and unique workflows to both the content building efforts and our software developers for the enhancement process. The integrity of our clinical content library is my responsibility.

Q. As in quality assurance?

A. Well, I do some consulting on the QA process, but I don't actually do the QA work. I'm either planning the clinical content or writing the clinical content and then reviewing it with our physician users. I do a lot more reading and writing and researching in ways that I never had time for in clinical practice.

SENIOR CLINICAL CONTENT EDITOR

Q. Sounds like you are quite content there. What was your biggest or toughest obstacle you had to face when you made your transition?

A. There were two. I actually now have to work harder than I did in clinic and I have a young son. The other was the financial risk of making the move. I'm heavily in debt with medical school loans and my ability to keep up with the payments is a big burden. The exciting part for me is that I have much greater potential for growth in this company and may someday actually get my medical school debt under control.

Q. And you've been in this position how many years now?

A. I started in January of 2009, almost two years ago.

Q. Starting to see some day light as far as your future financial picture?

A. Absolutely. There is great opportunity for me in this company and my hard work and commitment have already started to pay off.

Q. How was the response from your family and friends when you moved out of the traditional clinical setting?

A. People who were close to me were really excited for me because they knew that this would be a better fit for me. Now that they see how happy I am, they are all very supportive. It was hard to tell some people, like my sports medicine fellowship director, but even he turned out to be anything but disappointed in me. He admitted that if my year of fellowship training with him got me one step closer to what I was really meant to do, than he was glad to have been a part of it.

Q. Did you find any guiding principles or slogans as you were going through this transition?

A. The one that my coach Phillipa Kennealy shared with me: 'Don't move away from something, move towards something' has been the most powerful in this transition. It's a

Dr. Rebecca Winokur

positive spin that has helped me to move forward. Another that has been a help is: 'If you don't like something about your life, you are the only one who can change it'. Once I was open to change and had a vision for it, the universe responded and helped me find my way to where I am now.

Q. Now that you've gotten more experience in how to tap into that part of your body and mind, you can be more successful. Once you live over there it's a different picture for sure.
A. Definitely.

Q. You are going to present your story at the annual SEAK conference?
A. Yes, I'm looking forward to it. I've talked to a number of other physicians in various stages of their career transition. I know from my own experience how important it is to connect with other people who have been down the same path.

Q. Is there anything else you'd like to share about your current work?
A. I've been doing some development work for a non-profit organization, *Wide Horizons For Children*. They are working to break the cycle of poverty that leaves countless children orphaned around the globe. Their humanitarian and health care work in Ethiopia has been of great interest to me. I am in the midst of helping them to raise the funds needed to purchase two ambulances, one each for two hospitals that they are building in partnership with the Ethiopian communities where they will serve. It's been incredibly inspiring work and I am thankful that I can focus some of my spare time on this effort.

Q. I'm sure that what you bring back from that experience helps your clinical work as well? Just to have that outlook on life and the world must be powerful.
A. Yes and it has had a great impact on me both professionally and personally.

Q. What would you like people to remember you by after you've passed on?

A. I want people to remember that I lived a life of happiness, giving and no regrets. I felt like I had lost my sense of spirit in the clinic setting. I'm getting that back now and feel hopeful and happy again which is really important to me as I make my way through life.

DR. REBECCA WINOKUR

"You will become as small as your controlling desire, or as great as your dominant aspiration."

- James Allen

"When the winds of change are blowing, get your sail."
Dr. Brian Young, Medical Writer and Consultant

Southern charm, bred not copied, mingled with creativity and intense intuitive skills have positioned Dr. Young to deliver unexpected results in complex projects.

Possessing a very broad area of clinical experience; surgery and medicine, acute and chronic/rehab settings have added versatility and knowledge to his skill set.

Dr. Young has the "soft skills" that businesses have difficulty finding in employee candidates. Seeing grand possibilities, he seeks to bring them to fruition. Brian is a living example of the non-reverse engineer-able human asset which companies seek.

His primary areas of interest include health informatics, medical writing, and healthcare consulting.

Q. Where did you go to medical school?
A. The Bowman Gray School of Medicine, but I think it is now

called Wake Forest University Medical School--Bowman Gray Campus, graduating in 1985.

Q. Why did you go into medicine? Why did you want to become a physician?

A. I engaged in a lot of reflection and soul-searching throughout high school. I would get upset when I saw people with cerebral palsy or muscular dystrophy or some other disabling conditions. I wanted to understand what caused those conditions and eventually maybe even do research to fix those problems. Then also, I guess there was an overriding sense of wanting to help people. I wanted to understand the human body, my body, and how it functioned. I didn't want it to all be such a mystery.

It was passion infused with naive idealism, and even an overwrought perfectionism which wasn't perhaps the healthiest aspect of what drove me.

Q. What happened after that? What factors told you that you wanted to change your direction?

A. I guess the first seed of dissatisfaction came from my being naive and failing to fully apprise myself of the competitive nature of academic medicine and residency training. I thought once you got into medical school, you could become whatever kind of doctor you wanted to be, that you just picked what suited you and off you went. I soon discovered that was not the case.

By the end of my third year, I decided that ENT (Ear, Nose, and Throat) was where my interests and energies should be focused. Unfortunately, ENT was highly competitive with an early match program and unfavorable residency match statistics. The likelihood of obtaining a residency position in ENT worsened precipitously for each year following medical school. I tried to get into a residency program in ENT for three consecutive years after graduating, but was never successful.

The pressure to make a choice was served up quickly to me. I needed some income and I felt the pressure to start paying back my student loans. But I also felt I had no desirable options. Following that experience my career path in medicine turned into a downward spiral for me. I ended up in emergency medicine, which was problematic and not very satisfying.

I understand that there are people who like emergency medicine and are energized by it. I did not have that experience. It was exhausting. I understand that a physician can do some real good in the emergency room, and I felt like I did some real good there, but it wasn't enough to sustain me year after year.

Q. Did you do residency?
A. I did two years of general surgery residency as preparation for a residency position in ENT. There was a minimum of a one year general surgery requirement and some programs required two years prior to entering ENT training.

Initially, because of those requirements, it didn't feel like I was wasting time by doing general surgery. But, following the second year, I was coming up on the halfway point in general surgery. I was half way to the five years necessary to be a general surgeon. I just hated bowel surgery and that seemed to be what general surgeons were being relegated to via turf battles with surgical subspecialty areas. I just had no interest and so it didn't make any sense to continue along that trajectory. Moreover, I was not in the five year general surgery track at the University of Cincinnati, so continuing in general surgery was not an option for me anyway. I was there as one of the many surgical subspecialty trainees, meeting a one or two year requirement in general surgery prior to going on to a subspecialty training program.

So, I quit residency training and started working at a rural "freestanding" emergency facility, as well as doing house physician work and a little bit of urgent care center work.

During that period I made a decision to go back to school and get an MBA degree. I averaged 52 hours per week working in emergency medicine while attending graduate school full-time. I started in 1989 and finished my MBA degree in 1992.

Q. That's a big jump from cerebral palsy.

A. Boy! I'll say. I had a mentor in college, a biochemistry professor, who felt that if your research was keyed to the human condition, as opposed to the sex life of frogs, then it was somewhat more easily to get funded. That advice helped me make the decision not to pursue a Ph.D. and forever be dabbling in frog sex.

That was at a time when combined MD/Ph.D. programs were still nascent, so it seemed like I was going to have to structure something special for myself. Perhaps even "stack" a five year Ph.D. onto a four year medical degree program, all of which seemed to be insanely long and involved even to address and "cure" cerebral palsy. And so, I simply went to medical school. All along the way, I felt like I just kept making the whole Skywalker, "go to the dark side" choice. I kept chasing the money and the ego-funding prestige of being a doctor.

In retrospect, I should have continued to try and keep one foot in the research arena. That would have also helped with my present transition. I see other doctors who have transitioned, and their resumes are epic tomes full of research papers, patents, and board appointments. I just have to ask myself, "What have I done?"

MEDICAL WRITER AND CONSULTANT

Q. Well, it's different for all people. So you started to transition. I guess getting an MBA clearly demarcates that move. Was there still clinical medicine involved in your transition period?

A. No. Credentialing got to be an issue and I couldn't work in the ER without some sort of board certification. I returned to residency training in 1994 and did a three year hybrid internal medicine-primary care program at the University of Cincinnati. I then took my internal medicine boards and passed them in 1997. Then, suddenly the money jumped up several notches for me in ER work, so I kept doing that. Oh, the dark side.

From that point on, I feel like I was the poster child for professional burn-out and compassion fatigue in emergency medicine. I developed problems with alcoholism, going on into around 2000. Finally, after blowing two positive breathalyzer tests five months apart while working in the ER, I had to pull up the reins and say, "What is wrong with this picture?"

Part of the answer to that question for me was an understanding of my dissatisfactions with clinical medicine and patient care. I chose to surrender my medical license as a part of my recovery process and never returned to clinical practice. Since then I have embraced recovery and sobriety. I am coming up on ten years of continuous sobriety this December—a success story for me issuing forth from what originally felt like abject failure. So, to answer your question, I haven't practiced medicine since January 5, 2001. That was the last shift that I worked in an ER.

Q. I know that's huge. It's a very difficult situation. What do you have your sights set on now?

A. Well, I went to a SEAK conference to explore my non-clinical career options. After going through the groundwork of considering things like family support, ability to relocate, com-

DR. BRIAN YOUNG

pensation needs, further education or training needs, and using some of the conference tools, I felt best suited for careers in medical communications or healthcare informatics.

I liked the area of healthcare informatics because I love computers, the analysis of processes, troubleshooting, and leveraging information. Breaking things down into steps programming-wise or process-wise, whether it's project management or implementing electronic health records or computer programming, I got energized quickly by those activities.

On the other hand, there was a presentation which lumped medical communications, medical writing, advertising and promotion all together in one career category. I liked those areas for the potential for creativity. So, my career search became like a three pronged approach, the third prong is a non-medical, non-clinical interest in 3D design, prototyping, and CNC fabrication.

Q. That's exciting. You've found something distinctly different and non-clinical that you like. It seems like it's more of a game type of thing: informatics and computers and being creative and writing?

A. Yes, if I can break into any of those fields. Working a 24 hours on/24 hours off cycle in a single-coverage ER in a small county hospital felt like static drudgery to me. It just ran me into the ground. I know the grass is not always greener elsewhere, but there seems to be the potential for fun, as well as choice and creative freedom of thought compared to clinical medicine. It feels to me like the world of possibilities is open once again rather than running into the same building, seeing the same regulars in the ER and fighting drug seekers and all that misery.

I am now working with a mentor, Michelle Mudge-Riley, whom I met at the SEAK conference, to attempt to develop my "break in" strategy for my proposed career transition.

Q. Working with a mentor, how is that experience? I've heard tremendous things about Michelle. How is that for you? Has it been helpful?

A. It has been very helpful for me. I would highly recommend a mentor, or several. If anyone has reservations about it--just dive in and do it. The main thing it did for me was keep me on track, almost like homework assignments do in school. I tend to get lost in "analysis paralysis." But the deliverables for Michelle kept me on task. With those plus her professional skills and abilities, she is able to work in between the lines and see things that I do not see, just like a doctor would with a patient's health problems. It's like getting a continuous front end alignment. If I go on a tangent, she picks me right back up and sets me back on the goal-oriented trajectory of transitioning to a non-clinical career.

For starters, Michelle recommended I go to the Healthcare Information Management Systems Society (HIMSS) conference in Atlanta. So I went and shot my resume around, handed out business cards, went to the sessions and tried to get educated. I wasn't sure what it was like to actually be in healthcare informatics. I didn't want to project upon it things that were not true about the day to day work.

I'm still getting a sense of that. I'm still trying to follow-up with contacts I made there, to push out and see if I can gain employment. I haven't executed much on the medical writing side, but if it looks like I'm not going to be able to get anything in healthcare informatics, then I may move on to the other things.

Q. It seems like you hit a big obstacle with your substance abuse problem. Can you share anything tangibles from your transition?

A. Well, I am naturally proud of my recovery. I think if I can do

DR. BRIAN YOUNG

that without prior resume credentials, then there are a lot of other things I can do as well.

As far as other obstacles and subsequent breakthroughs, trying to self-promote and market myself with the skill set I developed as a doctor has been difficult. I had erected obstacles in my mind which made it really difficult for me to state how those skills were transferable to other non-clinical areas and how to represent that on my resume. It must have taken me two to three weeks of going over and over my resume, rewording it to try and anchor things that I had done as a resident, to skills and concepts which business people could connect to. That was a pretty huge breakthrough for me, although my resume is still not perfect.

Doctors are not often required to self-promote in that manner. It is a given in clinical careers that everyone more or less knows your skill set and its value and utility. Self-promotion quickly takes on a cheesy, used car salesman feel for me, so I do not do it well.

Once I finally started to connect on some of those issues, I thought, "You know, this really is not bull, I actually have these skills." It helped to have a physician mentor. It has helped as well to go out and try to self-promote, and to see that other people in non-clinical professions are actually rather receptive. In some regards non-clinical careers are a soft place to fall, because in business they are used to self-promotion. They understand. Those were breakthroughs that I had not anticipated.

It's scary at first, but once I saw that people were interested, I became less afraid. I have an active mind and I present myself well. I now detect that other professionals are willing to consider my transition to a new non-clinical career, to move outside of the physician archetype and do others things.

MEDICAL WRITER AND CONSULTANT

However, I have not made a successful transition just yet, and I am still running into some limitations and obstacles. For example, I was trying to move into vendor sales support in electronic medical record systems. I no longer maintain a medical license or board certification. It appears they require licenses in those candidates they deem viable for hire. I am wondering how to engineer around those limitations. Additional training or education, perhaps a certificate degree in informatics might help. Or perhaps I should move on to a different aspect of informatics—project management, implementation, consulting in the ambulatory sector—may be the approach.

Additionally, I have a huge gap in my employment history. That is very difficult to skirt around, but Michelle tells me it is not an absolute deal-killer. Michelle doesn't go to the pessimistic dark side of things as is occasionally my tendency—a nice counterbalance to have.

I think this transition to a non-clinical career is eventually going to take off. I started in earnest after the SEAK conference in October of 2009. It may take two or three years, if I decide to get another degree. Having the emotional stamina to tolerate a protracted career transition is definitely a must-have in my situation. I sometimes feel a sense of rejection, real or imagined.

Q. The SEAK conference is quite helpful. They definitely have a very comprehensive presentation. They know how to get things done. Do you feel like you are on your way now?

A. Yes, or I feel like I am now in motion though my path is frequently unclear. Before, I was an armchair physician-in-transition. Now I am doing something about it.

Q. How have your family and friends reacted to your transition here?

A. My wife has been very supportive. It has opened her eyes

DR. BRIAN YOUNG

as well, about how difficult it is for me to get a job, and that I may have to travel or relocate or take entry level positions to begin to re-path my career. With the SEAK conference, that was one of the pre-transition factors to look at, what kind of family support do you have? Often there are kids involved and schools and other family issues. I tried to do that processing work in and around the conference and after it as well in conversations with my mentor. I tried to do that and line it up. My family is supportive.

I think some of the people at the SEAK conference mentioned that their parents don't really understand. My mother is deceased, but my father has that "Marcus Welby" image of physicians in mind, what I call a country-club-practice archetype in his mind. He does not see any shortcomings in medical practice even though I bitch continuously about ER work. He doesn't understand, but he's 78 and he's not going to change. He saw a different era of medical practice. I don't try to sell him on it any longer, I just say, "You know what, I wasn't happy. I'm going to try to find a happier place and that is that."

Q. **Any advice you have for other docs contemplating major changes? Do you have any slogans you live by or principles that you would like to share?**

A. When you enter recovery, which is all about change, you quickly get to the concept that the only thing that has to change is everything. I started thinking about change a great deal in around early sobriety. I made up a slogan for myself: "When the winds of change are blowing, get your sail."

Then the other one I found on the back of a cereal box, where I commonly derive my philosophy of life. They had five quotes and you were supposed to match the quotes with who said each of them. I really liked one in particular because it gets at my need for unrelenting creativity and constant vexation over how things could be better. The quote was, "The future belongs to the creatively maladjusted." I think the thing that interested me the most was that Martin Luther King, Jr. was its author. I thought, 'Wow! That's pretty cool!' Those two slogans seem to casually edify me on a daily basis when I get in trouble or nervous about it all.

As far as advice, I think physicians should understand that they are inherently resourceful. We have to be in order to push the system to achieve quality care for our patients. I was nervous about where I was going to land after stopping medical practice while additionally having to enter recovery. It felt like jumping out of an airplane without a parachute.

There was a period of a few years where the anxiety was riveting. I felt lost and directionless. Occasionally, I still feel that way. But I try to remind myself how resourceful I am. Like a paratrooper, you can drop me out of the sky and I can land anywhere. Of course there will be that initial moment of bewilderment, but then I'll look around me and begin to marshall my resources. I just start putting the situation together.

My advice: Physicians are usually intelligent and resourceful. Approach the process of transition intelligently but fearlessly, because wherever you get to, there is always something you can do. There are always options and resources.

Try team building as you career transition. Make sure you have family support, get a mentor, network with people doing what you want to do. Put together your team. However, you have to do the work. You have to rewrite your resume, think about how your skills are transferable, and then formulate them into the language of sales or promotion. If you put all of that together as a unified approach to transitioning, you may not make millions of dollars, but I think the transition can be tolerable, less filled with anxiety and something

DR. BRIAN YOUNG

that you can own.

Q. Those are strong words Brian. So, when you get in transition you have to be moving. It's about energy.

A. That's the "get your sail into the wind" reference in my little slogan. Change is frightening to a lot of people. But, it's not something to be afraid of.

Q. Perhaps you can be an inspiration to others. Maybe one line will hit someone the right way, and change their lives.

A. Yes, every recovery is like that. You just move forward with your own process and speak with others about it, and people connect to it in different ways. You don't always know what connections will be made. They may find a word, a sentence, or a concept that triggers something in them.

I always feel like I don't have much to say, like I'm as cliché as a rock star on drugs. What is new or inspiring about that, it's been happening for years? Doctors constantly struggle with substance abuse issues. They stumble and fall. It's hardly the stuff of dreams. But then I remember my story is more about my recovery work and another slogan comes to mind, "You are not measured as a man by how you fall down, but by how you get back up." Everyone who gets back up, does it differently, and occasionally they do it with inspiring grace and panache, and, most of all, with hope. I hope one day these same descriptors are applicable to my journey.

ACKNOWLEDGEMENTS

I would like to acknowledge the efforts and help of the following wonderful, enthusiastic and helpful individuals.

Dr. Michelle Mudge-Riley (www.phphysicians.com) for referring so many interesting interviewees to me and also for writing a passionate and spectacular foreword.

Dr. Michael McLaughlin (www.prnresource.com) for making room on the bookshelf next to your landmark book, <u>Do You Feel Like You Wasted All That Training?</u>

Dr. Joe Kim (www.nonclinicaljobs.com) for your never tiring enthusiasm and referral stream.

Joy Heartsong (www.awakeningthetigerwithin.com), healing touch practitioner and author of <u>Awakening the Tiger Within: 9 Paths to Healing and Empowerment</u> for inviting me to the networking meeting in Denver where I met Brian Schwartz and started writing this book.

Dr. Kurt Kloss for finding that writing course for me.

Keith Lemons (Firefighter turned author) for always including me in your plans for success and never quitting on me.

To all my other family members and friends who kept asking how the book was coming.

I am truly grateful for this opportunity to share the stories of the 25 stars of this first volume. They each have so much to share. I hope you enjoy their journeys in transition.

- Richard Fernandez MD, MPH

ABOUT THE AUTHOR

Rich Fernandez, MD, MPH graduated from St. Louis University School of Medicine and completed his residency in Emergency Medicine at Washington University School of Medicine. Rich has been an emergency physician for over 30 years but always dreamed of being a full-time writer. In 2009, he officially began his transition to a writing career by starting Physicians in Transition: Doctors Who Successfully Reinvented Themselves. Rich lives in Colorado Springs, Colorado and can be reached at **rich@50interviews.com** and online at:

http://doctors.50interviews.com

ABOUT 50 INTERVIEWS

Imagine a university where not only does each student get a textbook custom tailored to a curriculum they personally designed, but where each student literally becomes the author!

The mission of 50 Interviews, Inc. is to provide aspiring, passionate, driven people a framework to achieve their dreams of becoming that which they aspire to be. Learning what it takes to be the best in your field, directly from those who have already succeeded. The ideal author is someone who desires to be a recognized expert in their field. You will be part of a community of authors who share your passion and who have learned first-hand how the 50 Interviews concept works. A form of extreme education, the process will transform you into that which you aspire to become.

50 Interviews is a publisher of books, CDs, videos, and software that serve to inform, educate, and inspire others on a wide range of topics. Timely insight, inspiration, collective wisdom, and best practices derived directly from those who have already succeeded. Authors surround themselves with those they admire, gain clarity of purpose, adopt critical beliefs, and build a network of peers to ensure success in that endeavor. Readers gain knowledge and perspective from those who have already achieved a result they desire.

If you are interested in learning more, I would love to hear from you! You can contact me via email at: brian@50interviews.com, by phone: 970-215-1078 (Colorado), or through our website:

www.50interviews.com

All my best,
Brian Schwartz
Authorpreneur and creator of *50 Interviews*

OTHER 50 INTERVIEWS TITLES

Additional topics based on the 50 Interviews model that have already been released or are in development:

Athletes over 50
By Don McGrath, Ph.D.

Successful Jobseekers
By Gordon Nuttall

Young Entrepreneurs
By Nick Tart and Nick Scheidies

Artists
By Maryann Swartz

Video Marketing Pioneers
By Randy Berry

Attraction Marketers
By Rob Christensen

Spiritual Leaders
By Tuula Fai

Actors
By Stella Hannah

Scientists
By David Giltner, Ph.D.

Wealth Managers
By Allen Duck

Millionaire Women
by Kirsten McCay-Smith

Entrepreneurs
by Brian Schwartz

Property Managers
by Michael Levy

Professional Speakers
by Laura Lee Carter & Brian Schwartz

Learn more at
www.50interviews.com